A WARRIOR'S GUIDE TO THE SEVEN SPIRITS OF GOD

PART 2:

ADVANCED INDIVIDUAL TRAINING

James A. Durham

xulon PRESS

A Warrior's Guide to THE SEVEN SPIRITS OF GOD Part 2: Advanced Individual Training
by James A. Durham

Printed in the United States of America

ISBN 9781613798478

Unless otherwise indicated, Bible quotations are taken from THE HOLY BIBLE, NEW KING JAMES VERSION. Original work. Copyright © 1979, 1980, 1982 by Thomas Nelson, Inc; THE HOLY BIBLE: NEW INTERNATIONAL VERSION®. NIV®. Copyright © 1973, 1978, 1984 by International Bible Society; and THE AMPLIFIED BIBLE. Copyright © 1954, 1958, 1962, 1964, 1965, 1987 by The Lockman Foundation.

www.xulonpress.com

TABLE OF CONTENTS

PART 2 - ADVANCED INDIVIDUAL TRAINING (AIT)

INTRODUCTION: xi

LESSON 1: Leading the Charge 29

LESSON 2: Recognizing the Victory 59

LESSON 3: Breaking up Pockets of Resistance 83

LESSON 4: Developing a Readiness Posture 103

LESSON 5: Exercising Self-Control 126

LESSON 6: Wearing Protective Equipment 149

LESSON 7: Knowing the Chain of Command 177

LESSON 8: Walking in Resurrection Power 204

SUMMARY 229

APPENDIX: 9 Principles of War 235

FOREWARD

In the military, soldiers who complete their basic training, move on to advanced training which is focused on a more individual basis. During my 29 plus years as an army chaplain, this phase of training was called "Advanced Individual Training" or simply AIT. This book was specifically written to further the training of those who have gone through the Basic Training in the first book of this series. However, it can also be read as a stand alone teaching on working with the seven Spirits of God.

As I said in the first book, I am convinced that spiritual warfare is being waged on a much grander scale than we have previously imagined. Battle lines have been drawn, and strongholds have been raised up and established. Unless we sharpen our skills at spiritual warfare and develop the gift of discernment to new heights, we will not be making a significant impact on the world or stemming the tide of the enemy's assaults on us, our families, our churches, and our communities. We have a great need for the gift of spiritual discernment in order to recognize the real enemy, and to see the movement of the Holy Spirit. We desperately need this discernment in order to keep within the flow of God's anointing in these perilous times.

We have lost cities, states, and entire nations to the enemy's persistent drive to take territory and deny God access to the hearts and minds of His people. It is time to get off of the defensive and go on the offensive. It is time to take the battle to the enemy. It is time to execute well planned attacks on his strongholds, and win back the territory for the kingdom of God. To accomplish this, we need well trained, knowledgeable, and courageous spiritual warriors to take the point and lead the charge. Perhaps you are one of these mighty men or women called by the Lord to take the lead. Perhaps, like Esther, you were raised up for such a time as this.

The purpose of this guidebook on spiritual warfare is to help these warriors see more clearly the resources provided by our Lord; to better understand the enemy and his tactics; to develop a strategy for responding to his attacks; and to move from defensive to offensive operations. We need to engage the enemy in his territory and inflict maximum damage on his forces as we significantly hinder his tactical operations. Our goal is to take back God's people, the nations, and His planet. Jesus came to destroy the works of the devil (John 3:8). As His disciples, it is our task to carry on his work.

ACKNOWLEDGEMENTS

I want to give first priority to thanking the Lord for the inspiration and help I received in completing this second book on spiritual warfare. Once again, to be honest, I must confess that the Lord deserves something over 99% of the credit. The first book evolved from a sermon series into a number of seminars and conferences as well as personal mentoring. During this time, a second series began to evolve, first as sermons and then as a book. I only completed three of the sermons in the series, but as the book was being written, I felt the inspiration of the Holy Spirit to add five more training sessions.

I also want to acknowledge the amazing help I received from my blessed and anointed wife, Gloria. Without her inspiration, encouragement, and assistance this book could never have been completed. I also want to acknowledge my daughter, Michelle, who was a constant and consistent cheerleader throughout the process. When I had any misgivings, I had only to turn to either of these two wonderful ladies for encouragement and inspiration.

I am grateful to Pastor Huh, Chul, Pastor of Pal Bok Presbyterian Church, and President and owner of Pure Nard Publishing Co. for encouraging me to complete this work in a timely manner and for providing venues for me to engage in teaching these lessons to the valiant warriors who bravely go into battle daily to stand against the enemy and build the kingdom of God.

INTRODUCTION

When soldiers complete basic training, the last thing they want to think about is more training. They feel like they have accomplished something really great, and they are now ready to take on the world. One group of basic trainees wrote a song which they performed in the dining facility after graduation. The song made reference to something which occurred over and over during their training. As they were standing around, someone would yell, "Make way! Make way!" When they hear this cry it was customary to move to make a path for someone important to come through their ranks. In the song, the graduating soldiers yelled at a group of drill sergeants, "Make way! Make Way! A soldier is coming through!" The graduating class loved singing this verse. And, the drill sergeants also liked the song, because it helped them feel like they had accomplished their mission of turning a rag-tag group of civilians into battle ready soldiers.

It is great to feel successful and prepared, however one reality of war is that you must continue to train in order to stay proficient in your skills as well as to continuously learn new ones. The same is true in spiritual warfare. We never get to the place where we no longer need to stay alert and learn. Yet, many believers have lapsed into a false sense of readiness. Advanced training was called for, but they did not respond. And tragically, after many years of service, they are still operating at the basic level. While the New Testament was being written, this phenomena of embracing a false sense of security had already emerged.

> *"Therefore let us go on and get past the elementary stage in the teachings and doctrine of Christ [the Messiah], advancing steadily toward the completeness and perfection that belong to spiritual maturity, Let us not again be laying the foundation of repentance and abandonment of dead works (dead formalism) and of the faith [by which you turned] to God, with teachings about purifying, the laying on of hands, the resurrection from the dead, and eternal judgment and punishment. [these are all matters of which you should have been fully aware long, long ago.] If indeed God permits, we will [now] proceed [to advanced teachings.]* (Hebrews 6:1-3, AMP)

The writer of Hebrews had a keen awareness that people had ended their training far too soon. They had stopped after basic training and falsely assumed that they were ready. But the author of Hebrews is determined to take them further into "advanced teachings." Now, it is your turn. You have gone through basic training for spiritual warfare, and it is time to move into your time of advanced training. Unfortunately many people today make the same choice as they did in at the time Hebrews was being written. They choose to avoid risks and stay in their comfort zone. However, in these last days, all comfort zones are an illusion. The enemy has deceived us into believing that we can have peace if we simply quit fighting and find a place to rest. This notion is part of his grand deception.

There are two compelling reasons why we must step out of our comfort zones and go into advanced training. First, it is because we are at war with an enemy who has already infiltrated our ranks and is daily working to destroy us. The second reason is more important and compelling. The Lord has called us out of the comfort zone and into the light. He has sent the Spirit of wisdom and revelation to make all of this clear to us. He has sent the seven Spirits of God into the whole world to lead us, fight with us, and fight for us. Now, we have no excuses for failing to move forward.

Many people like spiritual warfare. They like to learn about the spirits of the enemy and spend time fighting against them. For these warriors, it is a joy to see the demons being cast out, and victims being set free. Seeing people set free and rejoicing in their victories are good reasons to stay in the fight and improve our skills, but there is more. In this training, we will learn some advanced skills which will allow us to operate at a higher level and ensure that we keep the victory Jesus has already won for us. The lessons in this training were developed through the inspiration and guidance of the Holy Spirit over a period of more than two year. The titles of the lessons are listed below.

AIT 1: Learning to Lead the Charge
AIT 2: Recognizing the Victory
AIT 3: Dealing with Pockets of Resistance
AIT 4: Developing a Readiness Posture
AIT 5: Developing Self-Control (Self-discipline)
AIT 6: Wearing PPE (Personal Protective Equipment)
AIT 7: Understanding the Chain of Command
AIT 8: Serving in Resurrection Power

There is a very interesting phrase found in Numbers 21:14a (NKJV), *"Therefore it is said in the Book of the Wars of the Lord:"* Most people don't immediately connect with the idea of "the Wars of the Lord." The church has taught the doctrine of "peace at any cost" for so long that a misrepresentation of the Lord has emerged. People believe that God wants peace at any cost. This is simply unbiblical. Exodus 15:3 says, *"The Lord is a man of war; the Lord is His name."* These Biblical truths have not been consistently taught, and many in the church have grown up believing that the Lord no longer fits this "Old Testament" image. The people who make this claim have obviously not read the Revelation of John. Jesus will not return as a meek and lowly man of sorrows. He will return as a mighty man of war who will win a final victory over sin, death, the grave, Satan, and all enemies of Father God. He will be the King of kings and Lord of lords who rules with a rod of iron. The Word of God affirms that God does not change and that Jesus is the same yesterday, today, and forever.

What we need to understand about our amazing and awesome God is that He can maintain in perfect balance all of His various attributes. He can be the God who is love at the same time that He is the God of judgment and wrath. He is both the God of justice and the God of grace. He knows all things, yet chooses to forget our sins and trespasses. As we mature in the spirit, we begin to see that there is a season for every attribute of God. When we get confused, it is not His failure to be consistent, but our inability to understand the season we are in at that time. Remember: There is a time and a season for every purpose of God and it is true wisdom to be able to recognize the time you are in and what needs to be done in that time. The writer of 1 Chronicles gave praise for, *"the sons of Issachar who had understanding of the times, to know what Israel ought to do."* (1 Chronicles 12:32) Solomon had a clear understanding of God's times and seasons as he wrote Ecclesiastes chapter 3:1-8,

1. To everything *there is* a season,
A time for every purpose under heaven:
2. A time to be born, and a time to die;
A time to plant, and a time to pluck *what is* planted;
3. A time to kill, and a time to heal;
A time to break down, and a time to build up;

4. A time to weep, and a time to laugh;
A time to mourn, and a time to dance;
5. A time to cast away stones, and a time to gather stones;
A time to embrace, and a time to refrain from embracing;
6. A time to gain, and a time to lose;
A time to keep, and a time to throw away;
7. A time to tear, and a time to sew;
A time to keep silence, and a time to speak;
8. A time to love, and a time to hate;
A time of war, and a time of peace.

In the season of warfare, God is a "Man of War," and in the season of grace, He is the God of loving-kindness, mercy, and grace. Therefore, it should not surprise us when God started referring to His people as armies. Look closely at the two passages below from the twelfth chapter in Exodus, and see this shift in the character of God's people.

> *"And it came to pass at the end of the four hundred and thirty years—on that very same day—it came to pass that all <u>the armies of the Lord</u> went out from the land of Egypt."* (Exodus 12:41)

> *"And it came to pass, on that very same day, that the Lord brought the children of Israel out of the land of Egypt <u>according to their armies</u>."* (Exodus 12:51)

The Lord decreed that the people of the nation of Israel were now His armies. But, they were armies which were not yet ready for war. For this reason, the Lord began to give them training similar to what soldiers are taught today in boot camp. They learned to move forward at the Lord's command, and to stop their movements at His command. He began to teach them about making enemy estimates and establishing battle plans.

They learned about command and control, and developed battlefield skills.

> *"Then it came to pass, when Pharaoh had let the people go, that God did not lead them by way of the land of the Philistines, although that was near; for God said, "Lest perhaps the people change their minds when they see war, and return to Egypt." So God led the people around by way of the wilderness of the Red Sea. And the children of Israel went up in orderly ranks out of the land of Egypt."* (Exodus 13:17-18)

After more than 400 years of bondage in Egypt, the Israelites needed training, discipline, equipping, and leadership. They had not been trained to fight, and weapons had been kept from them for hundreds of years. None of the basic combat skills are taught to slaves for fear that they will revolt. However, as a free people, moving into a hostile region where they would encounter many enemy armies, they needed to learn quickly. They emerged from Egypt as a rag-tag band of ex-slaves, but entered the "promised land" as the trained and ready armies of the Lord. With each battle they gathered more weapons from the spoils of war, and learned how to use them very effectively.

In verse 17 of Exodus 12, God assumed command and led the people. As they experienced battle, and witnessed God's victories (especially the defeat of the Egyptian army) they developed a new understanding of who God is and what He is capable of doing.

> *"I will sing to the Lord, for He has triumphed gloriously! The horse and its rider He has thrown into the sea! The Lord is my strength and song, and He has become my salvation; He is my God, and I will praise Him; My father's God, and I will exalt Him. The Lord is a man of war; the Lord is His name. Pharaoh's chariots and his*

army He has cast into the sea; his chosen captains also are drowned in the Red Sea. The depths have covered them; they sank to the bottom like a stone." (Exodus 15:1-5)

It is at this point that we see God's new title ["*A Man of War*"] being used. Our God is a God who "triumphs gloriously!" He brought about one of the greatest military victories in history. He defeated one of the best trained and best equipped armies in the world at that time.

When God took command of His newly formed army, He began training them using "drill and ceremonies" which modern armies still use to teach soldiers to immediately and unquestioningly follow commands. In combat, soldiers need to respond immediately to every command. Some of these commands, which are key to winning the battle, put the individual soldiers at risk of being wounded or killed. People don't like to follow orders which put them in mortal danger. Obeying these commands goes against their innate survival instincts. To succeed in war, it is crucial to develop a culture of obedience which will result in a drive to obey which is stronger than the fear of death which tempts them to hesitate. This takes a great deal of training and discipline.

The first part of this training was called basic training or boot camp. All soldiers go through the same basic training. They are taught skills needed to survive on the battlefield, skills needed to combat the enemy, and skills needed to re-establish the peace after the hostilities cease.

In basic training, you first, learned to recognize the enemy situation and make an estimate of his forces, capabilities, and probable avenues of approach. During this phase of our training, you looked at the instructions Moses gave to the twelve spies. They were asked to report on specific things which are very similar to a current military estimate of the situation. Knowing the enemy's territory and capabilities is critical. You also learned to recognize some of the enemy's deceptive tactics used when he makes a move to get inside your camp where he is able to deceive some people into inflicting injuries on one another. Paul reminded the church at Corinth about Satan's deception.

> *"And no wonder! For Satan himself transforms himself into an angel of light. Therefore it is no great thing if his ministers also transform themselves into ministers of righteousness, whose end will be according to their works."* (2 Corinthians 11:14-15)

In other lessons, you learned about the importance of making an estimate of friendly forces. Remember this is where most groups make a critical mistake, because they do not factor God into their estimate. They don't consider God or other believers who are not from their denomination to be friendly forces who can be called upon to assist them in spiritual warfare. We need to get beyond our petty differences and work together to win this war. Make a special note to remember that God is a powerful combat multiplier.

In the final analysis, you learned and came to understand that God's seven Spirits are the answer to all of our spiritual warfare needs. In boot camp, you heeded the warning that the enemy will always send strong attacks when one of the Spirits is operating. The first response of many is to quit in hopes that this will cause the enemy to stop fighting and leave. However, you can't really leave the battlefield. The battle follows you wherever you go. The enemy's plan is the same whether you stand and fight or take flight. He is determined to steal, kill and destroy. He will attack whether you are armed or not. The only effective defense is a good offense supported by the seven Spirits of God. When the enemy attacks, you need to be prepared to fight and to release the full power of the Spirits of God.

Now, it's time to go beyond the basics of spiritual warfare. It is time to go on the offensive and take the battle to the enemy. Real warriors run toward the sound of battle, and not away from it. It is time for offensive operations.

During my officer training (ROTC summer camp), my group had been formed into an infantry company. The leadership positions were being rotated to give as many as possible the chance to experience leading in a combat situation. I had been in the role of a private for several hours and didn't really expect to be selected to lead the company. I was sitting in a foxhole, and out of extreme boredom, I began to reassemble an expended 60 caliber machine gun ammunition belt. Another soldier walked up, tapped me on the shoulder and said, "The company commander has been relieved and you have been selected to take his place." I was led back to the command post filled with shock and disbelief. I was given a quick briefing on our situation, and was told that my job was to lead a night withdrawal from our current position.

I took the radio operator on a quick reconnaissance patrol while I tried to remember the doctrine for a night withdrawal. I think I slept through part of that class. I took some toilet tissue out as we went on our patrol and hung strips on tree limbs along the way so that I could find the path back to my headquarters in the dark. In the distance, I heard the sounds of an ambush. The company going through the ambush was not prepared and did not do well. I knew at that moment that this would be my greatest challenge. So, I began to make action plans for the ambush. I put out the word that as soon as the ambush occurred, we would all immediately turn toward the ambush and attack with great violence. Everyone seemed to agree though we were not sure that this was the textbook solution.

When the ambush occurred, we executed our plan with such speed and violence that the cadre in the ambush panicked and ran into the woods. In the darkness, they ran into trees, bushes, and rocks causing several injuries. I received a good score for the unit's response, and for remaining cool during this event. Inside, I was anything but cool. I was terrified during the entire experience. But, I learned a couple of important lesson. You never know when you will have to assume a leadership position, and you need to prepare yourself well in advance. The other lesson was that you usually do not know when the enemy will ambush you, and it is wish to be prepared at all times.

In spiritual warfare, you may be called on to take a leadership role. In combat, leadership roles can change quickly. All those in leadership positions above you may be wounded, dead or incapacitated in a very brief period of time. The question to ask yourself is: Am I ready if I get called on to lead right now? The answer to this question will probably lead you to many other questions. Some key questions to ask are:

1. First, what do you need to do to become ready for leadership?
2. How do you prepare yourself in advance to handle the responsibilities?
3. Where do you go to get this kind of training?

The beginning point is to know the steps that a leader must take to accomplish his/her assigned mission. We are going to cover much of this during the training ahead. You need to practice continuously until your responses are virtually automatic. You don't have time to stop and think in the middle of an ambush or in the heat of an enemy assault. During these times, each decision is a matter of life and death, and must be made quickly. To be effective, you must stay current on the battle situation.

Military leaders refer to something called the "fog of war" (the confusion which takes over when the bullets start flying). In the fog, you are often out of touch with your leaders at higher echelons of command. These leaders may not be able to reach you and you may not be able to reach them for help in dealing with questions or to make calls for help. You may also be out of touch with many of your subordinate fighters. In these situations, you need to know what to do and when to do it. Are you ready now to take on these responsibilities?

Advanced Individual Training is also designed to assist people in developing military occupational specialties. Modern warfare is very technologically advanced, and many of the specialties needed to complete your assigned tasks take extensive training. This is true for training in spiritual warfare. We know that the Holy Spirit calls us to serve at different levels of ministry.

"And He Himself gave some to be apostles, some prophets, some evangelists, and some pastors and teachers, for the equipping of the saints for the work of ministry, for the edifying of the body of Christ, till we all come to the unity of the faith and of the knowledge of the Son of God, to a perfect man, to the measure of the stature of the fullness of Christ; that we should no longer be children, tossed to and fro and carried about with every wind of doctrine, by the trickery of men, in the cunning craftiness of deceitful plotting, but, speaking the truth in love, may grow up in all things into Him who is the head—Christ—from whom the whole body, joined and knit together by what every joint supplies, according to the effective working by which every part does its share, causes growth of the body for the edifying of itself in love." (Ephesians 4:11-16)

To complete this part of the task, you must find the answers to some key questions. Do you know your calling? Have you been given a specialty? Do you have a gift for it or do you need to develop your skills? Many of the specialized tasks require skills and gifts, as well as extensive training for soldiers to become proficient and effective. If you are in doubt about you specialty, ask the Holy Spirit to make it clear.

The Holy Spirit gives us the spiritual gifts we need for our assignment. We may desire other gifts, and that is okay. But, the key is to become fully functional in the ones you have already been given because these gifts are directly related to accomplishing the mission God has planned. These gifts often come at the point of need, and we must be ready to receive and use them at any time.

> *"There are diversities of gifts, but the same Spirit. There are differences of ministries, but the same Lord. And there are diversities of activities, but it is the same God who works all in all. But the manifestation of the Spirit is given to each one for the profit of all: for to one is given the word of wisdom through the Spirit, to another the word of knowledge through the same Spirit, to another faith by the same Spirit, to another gifts of healings by the same Spirit, to another the working of miracles, to another prophecy, to another discerning of spirits, to another different kinds of tongues, to another the interpretation of tongues. But one and the same Spirit works all these things, distributing to each one individually as He wills."* (I Corinthians 12:4-11)

From this passage, we know that there is a diversity of gifts. The Lord can give you any gift you need to accomplish His purpose. The Holy Spirit decides which gifts you receive and when you need to have them. There is also a diversity of ministries, and we are not all called to the same one. We are at our best when we are working in our own anointing in our assigned area of ministry. We are at our worst when we step outside our anointing or try to step into someone else's anointing. You must understand your calling, your gifts, and your anointing to be successful for the Lord. There is also a diversity of activities.

There are many different parts to a mission. Each part needs to be identified and someone with a unique specialty assigned to accomplish that portion of the mission. We need to learn to work together cooperatively as we do our part and support the gifts and responsibilities of others in our organizations.

Most people know the various pieces of the plan, but do you know how all of it fits together to equip you for your tasks? Do you clearly understand your assigned gifts, ministries, and activities? Now is the time to get it together. It is too late to work on these issues and get training after the shooting begins. You need to be wise, and prepare yourself now so that you are ready when the Lord calls you to duty.

Remember that the Holy Spirit is your sole source for all of these gifts and abilities. Take all your needs and concerns to Him. Even Jesus was unable to give the disciples everything they needed, because they were simply not ready to receive what he had to teach and train. So, the Lord sent the Holy Spirit to assist each of us in completing our training.

"I still have many things to say to you, but you cannot bear them now. However, when He, the Spirit of truth, has come, He will guide you into all truth; for He will not speak on His own authority, but whatever He hears He will speak; and He will tell you things to come." (John 16:12-13)

Jesus didn't have time to tell the disciples everything they needed to know. They were not ready to hear much of what they needed to receive and understand. In the same way, your pastor or teachers can't give you everything you need to know. You must rely on the Holy Spirit.

Are you ready for advanced individual training? As in all areas of spiritual warfare, we turn to the Lord for guidance and assistance. We acknowledge that the Lord is the supreme commander of all our allied forces. We know that He issues the orders, and our task is to follow them to the best of our ability. We know that it is the Holy Spirit who guides us into all truth and trains us to do the Lord's work. David understood clearly that it was the Lord who trained him.

"For who is God, except the Lord? And who is a rock, except our God? It is God who arms me with strength, and makes my way perfect. He makes my feet like the feet of deer, and sets me on my high places. He teaches my hands to make war, so that my arms can bend a bow of bronze." (Psalm 18:31-34)

David understood that it was God who equipped him for warfare. He knew it was God who gave him both strength and ability. It is important to remember that we serve this same God, who is a Man of War, and who trains and equips His soldiers for spiritual battles, today. David clearly understood that it was the Lord who was his protector and defender.

"You have also given me the shield of Your salvation; Your right hand has held me up, Your gentleness has made me great." (Psalm 18:35)

Paul took the concept further in the book of Ephesians. He identified the armor of God and our need to keep under its protection.

"Stand therefore, having girded your waist with truth, having put on the breastplate of righteousness, and having shod your feet with the preparation of the gospel of peace; above all, taking the shield of faith with which you will be able to quench all the fiery darts of the wicked one. And take the helmet of salvation, and the sword of the Spirit, which is the word of God;" (Ephesians 6:14-17)

Our God provides all we need to fight the good fight of faith. In addition to providing His protection, He has given us weapons of offensive warfare. He gave us the sword of the Spirit (the Word of God) as a powerful defensive and offensive weapon. Jesus taught us a great lesson in using this weapon in spiritual warfare when He resisted the temptations of Satan after coming out of His 40 days of testing in the wilderness. In Ephesians 6:18, Paul identifies for us another weapon of war, "praying always with all prayer and supplication in the Spirit, being watchful to this end with all perseverance and supplication for all the saints…" How many believers understand that praying in the Spirit is a powerful weapon for spiritual warfare. It has been given to you, so use it wisely.

Many of the lessons in Advanced Individual Training are not necessarily intuitive. God uses unusual means to accomplish great victories, and we need to be prepared to move with Him when He leads the charge. One great example is what Moses had to do in order to help Joshua prevail over the army of Amalek.

> *"Now Amalek came and fought with Israel in Rephidim. And Moses said to Joshua, "Choose us some men and go out, fight with Amalek. Tomorrow I will stand on the top of the hill with the rod of God in my hand." So Joshua did as Moses said to him, and fought with Amalek. And Moses, Aaron, and Hur went up to the top of the hill. And so it was, when Moses held up his hand, that Israel prevailed; and when he let down his hand, Amalek prevailed. But Moses' hands became heavy; so they took a stone and put it under him, and he sat on it. And Aaron and Hur supported his hands, one on one side, and the other on the other side; and his hands were steady until the going down of the sun. So Joshua defeated Amalek and his people with the edge of the sword." (Exodus 17:8-13)*

What does holding up a stick have to do with the army winning? God used the rod as a connection point for His power to flow to the army. God does not think or operate as the world does. We need the Holy Spirit to help us discern these truths. Most of us have been better trained in the ways of the world than in the ways of the Spirit. We need to set aside attachments to the wisdom of the world. We need to embrace the wisdom of God. We need to be open to learn new tactics and weapons which are unlike anything in the natural. We must learn to use the mighty weapons of the Lord.

"For though we walk in the flesh, we do not war according to the flesh. For the weapons of our warfare are not carnal but mighty in God for pulling down strongholds, casting down arguments and every high thing that exalts itself against the knowledge of God, bringing every thought into captivity to the obedience of Christ, and being ready to punish all disobedience when your obedience is fulfilled." (2 Corinthians 10:3-6)

We need to begin to do what we see God doing. We need to begin to say what we hear God saying.

If some of the thoughts and ideas presented in this training seem unusual or revolutionary, try to hold judgment until you have tested the ideas.

"For My thoughts are not your thoughts, nor are your ways My ways," says the LORD. *"For as the heavens are higher than the earth, so are My ways higher than your ways, and My thoughts than your thoughts."* (Isaiah 55:8-9)

I believe that it will facilitate your learning if you are able to consider the entirety of the teaching before judging the individual parts. May the Lord bless you with a renewed outpouring of the gift of wisdom and revelation! May He bless you with words of knowledge and words of wisdom! May the gifts of prophecy and interpretation be yours as you move forward in training and prepare to take back the offensive for the Lord! Amen and Amen!

NOTES

LESSON 1

"LEARNING TO LEAD A CHARGE"

O n the morning when I was doing the final editing on this chapter, I was given a vision of a very sophisticated war room in heaven. The walls were covered with widescreen, high definition monitors, and each was displaying the battle situation in a different geographical area. In addition to these screens, there were many control panels and communication devices. Our Command in Chief, 7-star General Jesus Christ, was conducting a meeting with the senior generals in His army. There were 25-30 leaders seated around a large oval shaped table and I saw rows of chairs for staff principles which were lined up in a gallery behind them. Every seat was filled and there was an air of excitement and anticipation throughout the room as everyone waited for the latest battle update and the issuing of orders for the day.

Jesus leaned forward and spoke in a very solemn voice, "I am going to ask some of you to lead the charge today. This will require great strength and courage. Some of you have the heart of a lion, and I can depend on you to follow this order. Some of you have not yet arrived at this level of courage, and I know that I cannot ask you to lead today. Pray that you may be filled with boldness and made ready for the battle tomorrow." I saw many in the room with right arms already tensed and ready to raise them to volunteer for the mission. But, Jesus wasn't taking volunteers, because He knew what was in their hearts. He knew whether they were ready or not. He knew which were lions and which were still lambs. I wondered how many of our spiritual warriors are really ready to lead the charge today.

I remembered the pictures and statues dedicated to infantry leaders. They were always jumping to their feet while the air was filled with enemy fire with a weapon in one hand and the other motioning toward enemy lines. These young warrior leaders were already a few yards out running toward the enemy and calling to the troops, "Follow me!" Jesus is looking for spiritual warriors who are running toward the battle and calling out to others, "Follow me!" This takes great courage. Soldiers have little respect for leaders who tell them to go into enemy fire, and they are hesitant to follow orders which may likely lead to their death. But a leader who runs to the battle calling others to follow inspires them to risk everything to follow. Soldiers willingly follow the one in the front who seems to be filled with great courage. I remembered the words of David in 2 Samuel,

"For You are my lamp, O Lord; the Lord shall enlighten my darkness. For by You I can run against a troop; by my God I can leap over a wall. As for God, His way is perfect; the word of the Lord is proven; He is a shield to all who trust in Him." (2 Samuel 22:29-31)

In the vision, I saw an expansive battlefield and from a position just above the center of our troops I was able to watch as one of those brave young warriors jumped up and called those with him to follow. As he ran toward the battle, he inspired courage in other leaders along the line. One by one they stood up, ran toward enemy lines, and called all those with them to

follow. It was as if we were witnessing another grand fulfillment of the words of David in 2 Samuel 22:34-35, *"He makes
my feet like the feet of deer, and sets me on my high places. He
teaches my hands to make war, so that my arms can bend a bow
of bronze."* With strength and courage, these young leaders and
those who followed them were taking the fight to the enemy.

I heard the Lord saying, "We can no longer tolerate our
troops hiding in fortresses while the enemy pillages the land.
We can no longer have warriors running to strongholds in the
wilderness to hide from the fight. We can no longer allow the
enemy to succeed in his war of attrition. Slowly, piece by piece
he is taking my territory because my people are afraid of the
fight."

Today, we need warriors who will pray for boldness like the
disciples in Acts 4:29-31,

*"Now, Lord, look on their threats, and grant to Your ser-
vants that with all boldness they may speak Your word,
by stretching out Your hand to heal, and that signs and
wonders may be done through the name of Your holy
Servant Jesus.' And when they had prayed, the place
where they were assembled together was shaken; and
they were all filled with the Holy Spirit, and they spoke
the word of God with boldness."*

Those who are willing to pray like this will be strengthened
in the Lord and enabled to make the affirmation David made
in 2 Samuel 22:40, *"For You have armed me with strength for
the battle; You have subdued under me those who rose against
me."* We must remember that it is the Lord's battle and He will
subdue the enemy forces.

An important maxim in the military is that every good
soldier needs advanced training. In the military, advanced
Individual training has several objectives. Four of the primary
goals are:

1). To help soldiers take their skills to a higher level;
2). To allow each soldier to develop a specialty in one or more areas while still maintaining the skills they learned during basic training;
3). To facilitate the building of self confidence in each trainee; and
4). For those who pass the test, to receive orders for their permanent duty station.

Warfare today is highly technical, and requires continuous training to get soldiers ready and ensure that they stay ready. One of the challenges for soldiers leaving basic training is maintaining what they learned during basic training. If there is a break between the basic and advanced training, soldiers often lose their edge on some of the skills. This is a particular challenge if some major holiday like Christmas or Thanksgiving occurs during that break and the soldiers spend an extended time at home with their families in a non-military environment. One of the skills which seems to degrade most quickly is saluting. This may go unnoticed until they meet the first officer at their new installation and forget to salute. At that point, they normally receive some very strong and painful remedial training. As soon as they meet their new drill sergeant, they normally get a refresher course on the proper wear of the uniform. They completed basic training feeling so good and so competent, and now they are rookies again being yelled at by almost everyone on the training staff.

As in the military, it is important that you maintain the skills you have developed for spiritual warfare. You may not have a friendly drill sergeant helping you to remember. So, you have to develop self-discipline to push yourself to keep studying your notes and reading your smart book (Bible). Many people take basic training in spiritual warfare, have fun looking at all the enemy spirits, celebrate the presence of the seven Spirits of God in their lives, and then promptly ignore everything they have learned. When an attack comes, they have to scramble quickly to find their notes so they can remember how to deal with a battle which has already begun. We simply must do better than this! Our Commander in Chief, 7-Star General, Jesus continually warned His soldiers to stay alert and ready. As obedient followers, we must do what Jesus told us to do. Stay ready! Be alert!

When soldiers arrive at their next duty station for advanced training, they normally receive another little green book called a CTT (Common Task Training) Manual. There was also another dreaded letter associated with this manual. It was another "T" which stood for testing. Every six months, soldiers are required to be tested on their ability to carry out the common tasks. Even chaplains have to go through the testing. I always had a challenge watching out for the subordinate chaplains. Chaplains are non-combatants and are not allowed to train on weapons or complete the testing phase for weapons. Some chaplains want to do the weapons training, and the leaders have to be diligent to ensure that they do not participate in this part of the test. The main point is: all soldiers, regardless of their branch of service, have to stay up to date on their training and be ready to deploy on short notice.

When I was assigned to the 121 Evacuation Hospital in Seoul, Korea, the commander required everyone to be trained and tested on common tasks. He believed that anyone in the army medical field who was not an expert in the basic skills of the military was unfit to serve. His goal was to help them get ready or to put them out of the Army. The doctors who had skipped this training and testing for a long time found out that the party was over. Many other soldiers from a variety of different branches of service had managed to get extended assignments in the medical command for the same reason. For those who had been hiding out in the hospital systems the message was: Welcome to the Army! You are a soldier first and then you have your medical or branch specialty.

If anyone didn't have the "Expert Field Medical Badge, this commander didn't want to see them or talk to them. That was a really huge change in the Army Medical Department. In addition, everyone in the medical command was required to have a CTT Manual on the top of his/her desk and be prepared to be tested at all times.

I remember watching this change take place first at the 121 Evacuation Hospital. Then, I observed this process continue to evolve as this commander was promoted three more times. With each promotion, he commanded larger groups and enforced the training and testing rules. After a short period of time, he became the commander of the Army Medical Education Department in charge of all medical training for the Army. He applied his principles to all medical training. At this point there was no way of avoiding CTT & T for people in the medical field. Finally, he was promoted to the top slot and became the Surgeon General of the Army.

Many soldiers at the 121 Hospital during his command thought he would eventually go away to some remote assignment and they could stop doing all this military training. After he became the commander of the entire Medical Command, they woke up to the stark reality that it was now required army-wide. This military commander knew a very important fact. If you are a doctor, nurse, or medic on the battlefield and you do not know how to do military tasks, you not only endanger yourself, but you also endanger the patients. All medical personnel must know how to protect their patients.

Every soldier must go through advanced training and receive a specialty. Each solider has a military designation to identify their specialty. It is called a military occupational specialty (MOS). Every soldier must have a MOS. One of the primary objectives of AIT is qualifying for and being awarded your MOS. Those who could not pass the test, had to be recycled or train in a different specialty. If they were unsuccessful again, they were likely to receive an 11B MOS as an infantry foot soldier. Being an infantry soldier is a rough, tough way to serve. Many soldiers were motivated to succeed in their advanced training, because they wanted to avoid being in the infantry. Other soldiers had infantry as their first choice. In the infantry, you are a war fighter and have to train all the time. As a chaplain in the 101st Airborne (Infantry) Division, I had to go with the soldiers on all their training missions, and it was tough. It is usually more difficult for chaplains because they are 10-20 years older than all the other soldiers in the unit. This type of intensely physical duty and training gets more challenging with age.

As a chaplain, I was also awarded an MOS after completing training at the Chaplain's School. With further training additional skill identifiers were added to the MOS so that anyone could check my military records to identify my qualifications for a new position.

As I mentioned earlier, warfare today in all branches of service is highly technical. The marines used to be called "leather necks" or "jar heads." They basically went out and destroyed lots of things and killed people. But today, they have so many sophisticated weapons and so many technological gadgets added to their tool kit, that marines must also be very technically skilled to be qualified for duty. As the weapons and tools become more technical, more training is required for every person in the military, and the need for readiness becomes more important because of the skills needed on the job.

An interesting phenomena is that the more ready you become, the more training you will receive. For example if you excel in infantry training, you may be selected for jump school. If you do very well at jump school, you may be selected for ranger training. If you excel in ranger training you may be selected for the special operations command. The more quickly you become trained and ready, the higher you are able to go.

Training and readiness lead to advancement, but advancement is never a reward for what a soldier has done, nor is it given for their glory or for their praise. In the military, you advance in order to be more useful for your branch of service and your local commander. Military promotions recognize potential for advancement to the next higher level. This does not mean the level where the newly promoted soldier will now serve. It is for the level just above the one they were promoted into. For example, if you are a captain and you get promoted to major, it is not just to allow you to serve as a major. but it also recognizes that the army leaders serving on a promotion board have seen your potential to function effectively as a Lieutenant Colonel. You are always promoted because of your potential to go to a level above the one they have just given you.

I believe that God promotes people in a similar way. He elevates you to a higher level because He sees your potential to go even higher. God promotes people who are "kingdom ready"! He promotes people who are capable of doing even more than their new position requires. He promotes you to give you a wider range of influence. This is something everyone needs to know as they progress through their advanced individual training. Perhaps this is a good time to ask the Lord about your potential for the kingdom of God. Do you have the potential to move up two levels today? If not, it is time for more advanced training.

WHAT IS YOUR POTENTIAL FOR THE KINGDOM OF GOD?

Another principle which is important to know is that those who are fearful simply don't advance. You cannot advance when you are easily overcome by fear. At this point, it is important to notice that no effective soldier goes into battle without some fear. The absence of fear is a sign of a character defect which may endanger the soldier and those around him/her. The army is looking for soldiers who can go into battle and fight effectively, because they have learned how to deal with their fear. They have learned how to use the fear to make themselves sharper, more aware, more focused, and more skilled in their area of operations. They have learned to use the fear to motivate themselves to do the training and accomplish the mission. However, if fear immobilizes you, you are useless in a military environment. And, you never know this about yourself or someone else until the bullets begin to fly. The presence of imminent danger elicits the strengths and weaknesses of your character. In this setting, you will see your best, but you will have to deal with your worse character traits.

In most military training programs there are times when you are around live fire. If a soldier is immobilized during training, they are not fit to serve in a real battle. Instead of being a combat multiplier, they will be a liability to the unit. Other soldiers will have to be taken off line to care for them during their episodes of fear and anxiety. To be an effective warrior, you must overcome your fear!

Fear is such an important element in war that the Bible addresses fear 253 times. And 206 additional times it mentions the word afraid. In the New King James Version, fear is addressed 459 times. In addition, we are told at least 84 times not to fear or be afraid. So, 84 times we hear God saying, "Do not fear! Do not be afraid!" In his second letter to Timothy, Paul addressed this topic and points to the source of the problem as being a "spirit of fear." It is more than an emotion. It is a messenger from the enemy who tries to oppress us with fear and prevent us from serving well in the Lord's army.

"For God has not given us a spirit of fear, but of power and of love and of a sound mind." (2 Timothy 1:7)

When you read scriptures about the power of God, I recommend that you read them aloud and put some power in your voice. Please read the above passage with passion and the power the Holy Spirit instills in you. It is important to be aware that when you are experiencing fear, God did not give it to you. If it didn't come from God, where did it come from? Answer: The enemy! In Romans 10:17, Paul teaches, *"So then faith comes by hearing, and hearing by the word of God."* I believe that fear comes by hearing the words of the enemy. I often teach people to read the Word of God aloud so that they can hear it, because hearing is the key to receiving it by faith. In the same way, if you confess the fear coming from the enemy, it will become more real and more effective in your life. So, confess what God says rather than what the enemy says. This way you will be able to operate in faith rather than fear.

People today make the same mistake as the ten Hebrew spies mentioned in Numbers Chapter 13. They over-estimated the power of their enemies, and spread their fear to the entire community! When you get ready to go into combat, you will hear many terrible stories from others which can lead you to fear. Before the "Desert Storm" operation in Iraq, people in the media began to talk about all the terrible things that might happen. They put a great deal of effort into making the American people fearful. Around the country, people started to build cemeteries to hold the thousands of casualties, but thank God, they never had to use them. The commentators were talking about the awesome power that Saddam Hussein had built up. They brought in alleged military experts who also promoted this fear. If you listened to and believed them, you probably thought we were walking right into the teeth of death, hell, and the grave. They talked about all the power coming against us and the awesome arsenal of the enemy. What a waste of time and energy that turned out to be.

After declaring over and over that we were going to face the "mother of all battles," Saddam Hussein ran to find a hole in the ground to hide in as soon as the battle began. Many American people fell for all this useless hype, and fear ran rampant in our nation. When our forces moved onto the battlefield all of Saddam's alleged "elite Republican Guard" units began to collapse like toppling dominoes. They were running as fast as they could run, but couldn't outrun the munitions coming at them.

We do the same thing in the spiritual realm. Like the Israelite spies, we give too much credit to the power of the enemy, and begin to built fear which many lead to people running away instead of standing to fight. I hear people talking constantly about their battles with Satan and how powerful his forces are. They just give too much credit to the power of the enemy. What these people end up doing is confessing the power of the devil instead of the awesome and overwhelming power of God. If you fall for this deception and start confessing the power of the devil, you are going to get overwhelmed by it. When you attribute power to him, you are in reality empowering him to overwhelm you with fear.

If you leave the power of God out of your life, the alternative is to be filled with weakness and fear. Only two of the twelve spies factored God into their estimate of the situation. They were the only ones who even thought about God when they made their assessment. Ten of the twelve spies went into panic mode and began to confess, "There are giants in that land, and we felt like grasshoppers in their presence! The cities are fortified, and it is a hard land. We think we just need to pack up and go somewhere else before it's too late! Forget about the milk and honey. Let's put some distance between us and them." How many of us do the same thing on a daily basis? I hear the same thing from people all the time who are claiming to be intercessors and warriors for the Lord, but confessing that they are being defeated by the enemy.

Take a moment to look at Caleb! He began to praise God, to honor God, and to testify about what God could do. Caleb never let fear control his circumstances. When he was in his 80's (over 40 years later), he was still filled with faith in God. He proclaimed that he wanted the hill country were the giants lived. He still had the same fight in him that he had when he was forty years old. There is an old country saying: "It's not the size of the dog in the fight, but the size of the fight in the dog!" Caleb was still full of fight, and he went into the land and routed those giants which the others had feared. When this 85 year old man of war came into the land, the giants ran in fear for their lives. That's what happens when God is with you in the battle. Remember that God and you make an awesome team. He is awesome and allows you to be on the winning team. So, why should you fear?

The Bible repeatedly stresses the point that we must overcome fear through our faith in God. And, I sometimes wonder, "When are we going to get it?" We need to know — that we know that we know — that God's power is infinitely greater than any power the enemy may possess. We need to proclaim with all our might, "We have a great and awesome God who is much bigger than the devil!" Hallelujah! It is important to proclaim these things aloud and build up your most holy faith and confidence. Confess it over and over. Then add another confession to it. "Compared to God, the devil is a tiny little demon who trembles in the presence of my all powerful Father God!' Hallelujah! Confess it over and over so that you can get over your fear of him. Fearing the devil is disobedience to the Lord. He commanded us not to be afraid.

> *"Therefore submit to God. Resist the devil and he will flee from you. Draw near to God and He will draw near to you. Cleanse your hands, you sinners; and purify your hearts, you double-minded. Lament and mourn and weep! Let your laughter be turned to mourning and your joy to gloom. Humble yourselves in the sight of the Lord, and He will lift you up."* (James 4:7-10)

How big is the fight you need to have with the devil to win and keep your victory? All you have to do is resist him and he will flee. If he is fleeing from your faith, how big can he be? You don't have to fight. You just need to show up and resist him. Then this passage from James challenges the fearful to clean up their act; to stop being double minded (claiming faith and fearing the devil); and mourn for their failure to trust God. Verse 10 then reinforces verse 7 which calls for us to submit to God. Here we see that if we humble ourselves before God, he will lift us up before the devil.

The Bible gives some awesome illustrations about how this works. Over and over in the Bible we see God lifting people up. But, you never see Him lifting up those who are proud. Pride tells us that we can do it on our own, and that we don't need God. Humility recognizes our dependence on God, and positions us to receive His favor. One of my favorite illustrations of this belief in the power of God is seen in the story of King Jehoshaphat in Second Chronicles.

JEHOSHAPHAT LEARNED TO LET GOD FIGHT HIS BATTLES

Jehoshaphat was a good king, but in spite of his goodness, this vast army came against him. Three nations had gotten together to come against Israel in an attempt to drive them out of the land and destroy as many of them as possible. From the human point of view, it seemed hopeless. As the Israelites looked out at this vast army, they knew that there was no way to defeat them with their own power. So, what did Jehoshaphat do? First let's look at what he didn't do. He didn't let fear break his spirit. He didn't get into panic mode and try to run and hide. He took it to the Lord. He decreed a time of fasting and prayer. He went before the Lord, and laid out the situation to Him, and asked the Lord to tell him what to do. Because of his humility, faith, and submission, the Lord sent an answer to him through a Levite named Jahaziel.

"Then the Spirit of the Lord came upon Jahaziel ... a Levite and descendant of Asaph, as he stood in the

assembly. (He was just standing there when this was happening, and the Spirit of God came upon him) He said: "Listen, King Jehoshaphat and all who live in Judah and Jerusalem! This is what the Lord says to you: 'Do not be afraid or discouraged because of this vast army. For the battle is not yours, but God's." (2 Chronicles 20:14-15)

Have you ever noticed that when God tells people not to be afraid, they're already petrified with fear and most are trembling as their weak knees knock together. Sometimes, it seems like God has a sense of humor in these situations. People are standing there trembling in fear, and God says, "Don't be afraid!" Once again, we see that fearful people just don't realize how big God is.

This is another good place to make your affirmations again about how big God is. Say it out loud filled with confidence. We need to really get this idea locked into our hearts and minds. Too many people seem to see a big devil and an almost equal sized God. When they look at things this way, they begin to say, "Well, we're in this great big battle, and who knows how things are going to go whether the winner will be the devil or God?" We need to stop looking at things this way. We need to start seeing situations through the eyes of faith, and understand how big God really is. How big is God? He not only kicked the devil out of heaven, but he also kicked a third of the angels out with him because they had joined in his puny little rebellion. As far as I can tell, God didn't even work up a sweat when he threw them out. They were out of heaven and the door was locked behind them. They can't even go back for a visit. This battle in heaven was not a close call or a struggle between two nearly equal spirits. It only lasted a nanosecond and the devil was flung like lightening to the earth. What you need to be able to see at all times is A GIGANTIC GOD and a tiny little devil. It is time to get back to faith and back into the fight.

It seems as if God has to constantly remind us of who is actually under attack. He has to repeatedly teach His people whose battle it really is. The prophet, Jahaziel, proclaimed that this was not Jehoshaphat's battle but God's battle. And it is important to realize that every battle with the devil is God's battle. The devil is trying to steal what belongs to God and then kill and destroy the Lord's people, purpose, and plans. Can he do that? Not without our permission. When an attack comes, too many of us take it personally. We think it is all about us, and wonder how we can possibly overcome the forces against us? With whiny voices we begin to cry out in weakness. "Oh man, why is this happening to me? How am I ever going to deal with this? Lord, can't you see all these people coming after me? I just don't know what I'm going to do. It is just so terrible! Oh, poor me! Poor me!"

Instead of all that whining and begging, we need to remember what the prophet said to Jehoshaphat: "It's not your battle! It is God's battle! Once again, we are at a great place to make some of our decrees out loud with voices of conviction and faith, "It's not my battle! It's God's battle!"

Isn't this what David did when he went to visit his brothers who were fighting the Philistines. Everyone in Israel was trembling in fear because of this one giant. In essence David said, "What's wrong with you! Don't you understand? This is not your battle! This is God's battle!" David volunteered to go fight the giant by himself. Somehow that same fearless spirit which was on Caleb was now on David. They tried to put all of Saul's armor on David, but he could not even walk while he was wearing it. David said, "I don't need all that armor. Just give me my little sling shot, some stones, and a stick. He took five stones. I believe he did this because Goliath had four brothers. He was ready in case they showed up to help their brother. And the Bible shows us what happens when a young boy armed with a stick, a slingshot, five stones, and God can do to a giant who was the champion of an entire enemy army.

You must stop looking at things from the human perspective in the weakness of your flesh. You must stop getting caught up wondering what you are going to do! Do the same thing Jehoshaphat did! Take it to God! Lay it out before Him. When you get the proper perspective (this is not my battle but the Lord's battle), and you get connected to His power the situation changes. When you see things this way, it takes a lot of the pressure off of you. There is no need for fear, because God is able, God is in control, and God can handle the devil. It is not even a close contest. Let's look again at the account in Second Chronicles and see what the Lord said through the prophet Jahaziel.

"And he said, "Listen, all you of Judah and you inhabitants of Jerusalem, and you, King Jehoshaphat! Thus says the Lord to you: 'Do not be afraid nor dismayed because of this great multitude, for the battle is not yours, but God's. Tomorrow go down against them. They will surely come up by the Ascent of Ziz, and you will find them at the end of the brook before the Wilderness of Jeruel. You will not need to fight in this battle. Position yourselves, stand still and see the salvation of the Lord, who is with you, O Judah and Jerusalem!' Do not fear or be dismayed; tomorrow go out against them, for the Lord is with you." (2 Chronicles 20:16-17)

This reminds me of the way things go in battles today. Soldiers who are deployed to a war zone line up against the enemy. When they look out at the enemy forces, it may be frightening. But, what they may not realize is that several hours ago some airplanes took off from an airstrip in Missouri. And suddenly, B-52 bombers fly over. They are flying at such a high altitude, the enemy may not even notice them or hear them. And, suddenly, they carpet bomb the entire area occupied by the enemy. The whole area in front of our soldiers comes alive as hundreds or sometimes thousands of little bombs go off almost simultaneously. There is nothing in front of their position but death and devastation. When the dust clears, they look, but they can't see the enemy. Those who have survived the bombing are likely to be so disoriented that all they are able to do is crawl into holes and caves with the sole objective of trying to survive.

God's power in war is a little like this only much bigger and more powerful. He comes on the scene and carpet bombs the devil and his forces. The effect of God's intervention brings such shock and awe to the enemy forces that those who survive often turn on one another and complete the job of self-destruction. When God reveals his plans to people, they are often confused, because He has such unusual methods of operating. We have to remember that God doesn't think like we think and He doesn't fight like we fight.

GOD GAVE JEHOSHAPHAT
AN UNUSUAL BATTLE PLAN

God does this over and over in the Bible and people always seem to be surprised by His methods. They begin to think in human terms and worry about getting organized, getting plans published, and getting into agreements with others. They think they have to manage the plan in order for everything to work properly. Then God intervenes and gives us a plan that to most people seems a little silly. We need to learn how to trust him and remember that none of His words ever come back to Him void. He always accomplishes His purpose. Let's look back at Second Chronicles and see the plan God gave to Jehoshaphat.

"So they rose early in the morning and went out into the Wilderness of Tekoa; and as they went out, Jehoshaphat stood and said, "Hear me, O Judah and you inhabitants of Jerusalem: Believe in the Lord your God, and you

shall be established; believe His prophets, and you shall prosper." And when he had consulted with the people, he appointed those who should sing to the Lord, and who should praise the beauty of holiness, as they went out before the army and were saying: "Praise the Lord, For His mercy endures forever." (2 Chronicles 20:20-21)

Jehoshaphat's lead element was the worship team. Can you imagine doing that today? I like to think through these unusual occurrences in scripture and put them in a modern context. I like to imagine how the praise team would feel and react if you asked them to be the lead element against an army of almost 200,000 soldiers. How would most of them react if you asked them to carry musical instruments instead of weapons to lead the charge? It takes a great deal of faith to follow many of God's plans. Do we trust Him enough to do what He says? For those worship warriors who accepted the challenge, the words of their battle song had already been written in advance. They went out singing, "Give thanks to the LORD, for his love endures forever." This is a victory song, and they were told to sing it before the battle. I like the idea of going into battle so confident of our victory that we are singing songs to praise God for getting us through it before the first bullet is fired. Imagine how this affects the enemy. He sees the people of God coming against him singing victory songs as they draw up to the battle lines. We expect to sing victory songs after the battle is won and often miss the power that God releases through His praise. If we trust Him enough, we will begin to see, there is some awesome power in our praise and worship.

Look again at 2 Chronicles 20:22, *"Now when they began to sing and to praise, the Lord set ambushes against the people of Ammon, Moab, and Mount Seir, who had come against Judah; and they were defeated."* It's so easy to just read these stories and take everything for granted. It may just seem normal because you have never been in a situation like this. But, notice that in this situation the promise of God is activated by their action. They had to first step out in faith before God's plan went into action.

This reminds me of the Jordan River crossing when Israel went into the promise land. It was the rainy season, and the river was at flood stage. Water had overflowed all the banks and was raging in the middle of the surging stream. Then, Joshua took his position and commanded the people to cross over this raging river. Can you imagine the hesitancy? I can almost hear them saying, "You want us to cross a raging river by foot? Yeah! Right! You've got to be kidding!" When Moses parted the sea, the wind blew all night and dried out the bottom, and they didn't go in until the ground was firm. But, this time, they had to step into the water first. And, as soon as the priests who bore the ark stepped into the water it piled up in a heap upstream from them. They had to activate the promise by their actions. Again, notice who was sent into battle first. The priests carrying the Ark of God were the lead element.

Jehoshaphat, his army, and the praise team had to do the same thing. They had to step out in faith before God's power was released. They had a prophetic word, but it didn't manifest until they began to worship. Have you ever wondered how many prophesies spoken over you haven't manifested yet. It may well be because you have not activated them with your step of faith?

"Now when they began to sing and to praise, the Lord set ambushes against the people of Ammon, Moab, and Mount Seir, who had come against Judah; and they were defeated. For the people of Ammon and Moab stood up against the inhabitants of Mount Seir to utterly kill and destroy them. And when they had made an end of the inhabitants of Seir, they helped to destroy one another."
(2 Chronicles 20:22-23)

This is the kind of battle I like to participate in. But, too often we get caught up in trying to do it ourselves in our way. Have you noticed how many intercessors get caught up trying to learn a new strategy to deal with the enemy. They work so hard on developing their plans and organizing their actions. When, all they have to do is worship the Lord. I want you to take note that one of the advanced skills in advanced individual training is worship.

It may sound strange to call worship an advanced skill. Let me explain. When you first became a Christian, you didn't really know how to worship. You see this still happening all the time. People come into the worship service wanting to worship, but they don't know how. They sing songs that sound good and they feel good doing it. They say prayers that sound good and they feel good. They may memorize some verses from the Bible that sound good and feel good. But, in the beginning, they are just imitating the worship they see in other people. But a time comes as they develop their relationship with God when they learn how to truly give Him worship. When this happens, their entire experience of worship shifts to a much higher level. A transformation has occurred, and there is now power in the worship. As they worship in power, the atmosphere begins to shift, and the glory of God comes in. When this happens, the enemy flees, and true worship begins to flow with the power of God.

When you give sincere praise and worship to the Lord, it releases great spiritual power into the atmosphere. Demonic spirits don't like real worship, but the angels of God do. When the angels of God begin to show up in worship, the demons have no choice but to flee. When a battle is won like this one, through the power and direct intervention of God, the enemy becomes fearful.

"And the fear of God was on all the kingdoms of those countries when they heard that the Lord had

fought against the enemies of Israel. Then the realm of Jehoshaphat was quiet, for his God gave him rest all around." (2 Chronicles 20:29-30)

In this passage, we clearly see that much more had happened than just winning a battle. Most of us have noticed that when we fight our own battles, the victory only last for a little while. Then the enemy comes back, and we have to fight again. This may happen over and over again. But, when you let God fight the battle, the enemy scatters. The result is that you see the enemy forces, in the confusion and FOG of war, inflict great casualties on their own forces. After God wins a battle like this, the enemy doesn't come back for a second helping of defeat. Other enemy forces hear about the outcome and they don't want to experience the same disastrous outcomes. At this point, God gives you rest on all sides.

Remember the Seven Spirits of God from the boot-camp training. The Lord releases those seven awesome and powerful Spirits into all the earth. God has done this over and over throughout history. He brings His awesome power to bear on your situation through these seven Spirits, and the enemy is certain to flee.

When the Israelites came out of Egypt, the power of God was with them. It was visibly present in the cloud by day and the column of fire by night. That power of God held Pharaoh and his army away from Israel all night while God's power working through Moses caused the waters to part and the bottom of the sea to dry up. God's power was there to let them cross over the sea in safety. The dry land they walked on became mud and the chariots bogged down. While the army was held in place God's power brought the water of the sea down on the Egyptian army. The people didn't have to do anything. They just stood by and watched God win the battle for them.

We see the same power of God fighting the battles in the lives of David, Hezekiah, and Jehoshaphat. Yet, the people of

Israel had trouble trusting God. They always needed a strong and faithful leader to keep them built up and strong in the Lord.

And the same thing can happen to us when we are faced with spiritual warfare. In spite of all we have seen God do in our lives, we may have trouble trusting God for the next battle. We need to remember that the same power of God which won victories in the past is still available today. Trust Him to do for you what He did for them. This is one of the advanced skills — to learn to trust God. It sounds basic, but most people never get to this place of trust. Their faith and trust is weak because they don't exercise them continually. It has been said that faith is like a muscle. It gets stronger with exercise. Faith also gets more powerful with confession. I encourage you to confess it now and confess it often. Proclaim with power and authority, "I'm going to trust God! He has always been faithful to me, and I know He always will be faithful to me! So, I am putting my faith in Him!" Amen? Hallelujah!

Now, let's take our faith to a higher level of trust. Don't merely trust that He can do things for you, but trust that He will do them! For example, faith doesn't have to do with believing that God can heal you, but true faith trusts that He will heal you. You can even take faith to another level by believing that He has already healed you and you are just waiting for it to manifest in the natural. Faith sees things in the spiritual and trusts absolutely in their manifestation in the natural.

Whatever you may be facing, take it to the Lord, and let Him fight His battles. Your task is to give Him praise and worship. Once again, it is important to learn to confess power statements with strength and authority. I get tired of weak and wimpy prayers. I don't like half hearted affirmations. I encourage you to practice putting power and authority into your voice with all your affirmations. The first part of Psalm 8 is somewhat gentle when you affirm your love for the Lord, but the rest of it should be read aloud as power affirmations.

"I will love You, O Lord, my strength. The Lord is my rock and my fortress and my deliverer; My God, my strength, in whom I will trust; My shield and the horn of my salvation, my stronghold. I will call upon the Lord, who is worthy to be praised; So shall I be saved from my enemies." (Psalm 18:1-3)

We need to read this psalm with power and authority because these are affirmations about our awesome God in whom we place all our trust.

HE IS MY ROCK!
HE IS MY FORTRESS!
HE IS MY DELIVERER!
HE IS MY REFUGE!
HE IS MY STRONGHOLD, AND HE IS WORTHY OF PRAISE!

Remember that one advanced skill to develop in your advanced training is to learn to praise Him before the victory is won. When you first hear that a battle is about to begin, start praising Him for winning the battle. That is trust! That is faith. It is believing that He will win, and not just that He can win. When the Lord hears you praising Him in faith, He sets up ambushes for the enemy. When you are in the military, you just hate ambushes. They are no fun at all. If you are moving along with your group and suddenly get attacked, the shock factor can be overwhelming. And when God sets up an ambush, you can be certain that it will overwhelm the enemy and throw them into shock and debilitating fear.

So, you need to be careful to give Him all the praise before the battle, because this releases Him to set up those ambushes for you. And you will give Him all the credit, all the praise, and all the glory afterward as well. You must learn to avoid taking any credit for the victory before or after the battle. You must affirm again and again that it was God who did it. When you learn to do this, you will continue to build up your faith and trust. By doing this, you will be enabled to stand in faith and in readiness for the next victory. Remember how David used to say, "I will lift up your name and praise you in the assembly. I will declare to everyone what you have done! I will give you the glory forever!" This is an advanced skill you need to develop and practice on a daily basis.

Always remember that worship is the answer to every situation you will have to face. Have you seen those bumper stickers that say, "Jesus is the Answer!" I remember some critics who asked, "What is the question?" People of faith affirm that Jesus is the answer to all of life's big questions. And, I want you to know that worship is the answer for any problem or hardship you may have to endure in the future.

WHATEVER YOU ARE FACING
WORSHIP IS THE ANSWER

Worldly wisdom says that this is foolishness. Remember the old adage, "Don't count your chickens before they hatch!" Worldly wisdom says that seeing is believing, but we say that believing is seeing. Remember Hebrews 11:1, *"Now faith is the substance of things hoped for, the evidence of things not seen."* You need to see things in the spiritual realm before they manifest in the natural. So, you have to decide who you are going to listen to. Are you going to listen to the wisdom of the world or are you going to listen to God's Word? Each of us must make this choice for ourselves. But, the sooner you see whose battle it is, the faster you will be able to respond in the appropriate way.

Training and practice allow you to respond appropriately in a difficult situation. You become a good soldier through constant training and practice. Every time you face a very small problem, put your training into practice. The best way to learn how to deal with spiritual warfare is to begin with tiny problems and work your way up to bigger ones. Don't wait for something really big before you try out your skills. When something really big happens, you are likely to be overwhelmed and have a tough time remembering your training. So, start with something small. Respond by immediately going into worship. Be encouraged when you see your worship release God's power to break off the attack or cancel the problem. Celebrate when you see God move in and establish ambushes against the enemy. Gradually you learn to make worship your first response. Then you become ready to handle larger and larger problems.

When you are hit by the enemy's worst, you know that worship will get your through it. You already know what the enemy plans to do. According to John 10:10, he comes to steal, kill, and destroy. When the enemy tries to steal your health, your money, your friends, or steal your loved ones away from you, don't panic. Just worship the Lord and wait for Him to guide you. When the enemy tries to kill you, your relationships, or your love, don't panic. Just worship the Lord, and ambushes will be set up for the enemy. When the enemy tries to destroy your work, your joy, or your glory, don't panic. Just begin to worship the Lord, knowing that it is actually His battle. Amen? WORSHIP is the answer. Worship is the first response needed in every enemy attack.

> *"Why are you downcast, O my soul? Why so disturbed within me? Put your hope in God, for I will yet praise him, my Savior and my God. My soul is downcast within me; therefore I will remember you from the land of the Jordan, the heights of Hermon—from Mount Mizar. Deep calls to deep in the roar of your waterfalls; all your waves and breakers have swept over me."* (Psalm 42:5-7, NIV)

Deep calls to deep, and when you are going through something deep and find that your soul is downcast what do you do? You remember God and begin to praise Him. Remember who He is, what He can do, what He has done in the past, and what He has promised to do in the future. When you remember God, it totally changes your outlook and your circumstances. When you get into fear, you're telling God you don't think He's big enough. You're telling God your problems are too big for Him. You're telling God you don't think you can trust Him this time. When you react in fear, you will probably get a response from God, but it may not be the response you wanted. You must learn to respond with worship! Begin to quote the Word of God and build up the faith that will vanquish fear. That's what David learned to do.

> *"When I am afraid, I will trust in you. In God, whose word I praise, in God I trust; I will not be afraid. What can mortal man do to me?* (Psalm 56:3-4, NIV)

I recommend that you read this passage several times aloud with authority based on your most holy faith. Store it in your heart so that when fear comes, this will be your immediate response. Our training has taught us that the Word of God is the Sword of the Spirit. When you say these power passages over and over, you store them in your heart. This is a sword drill. When fear comes, you draw out the Sword of the Spirit and vanquish all fear with the Word of God.

Praise and Worship help you to get your focus back. They will give you a new perspective on the truth about your problems. Worship will help you to remember that this is God's battle and He is ready to fight as soon as you release him and give Him authority over you battles. You do this through your worship. As you worship, you build up your relationship with Him. You become stronger and better prepared to serve on God's team.

Remember that when the enemy attacks you, he doesn't really care about you. He wants to stop what God is doing. When you finally realize this, it will change the way you look at every situation. You will begin to see that in addition to releasing God's power, you are also building yourself up. Praise and worship build up your faith. The more you worship the Lord, the stronger you become. Remember Joel 3:9-10:

"Proclaim this among the nations: "Prepare for war! Wake up the mighty men, let all the men of war draw near, let them come up. Beat your plowshares into swords and your pruning hooks into spears; Let the weak say, 'I am strong.'"

When the weak begin to proclaim that they are strong, they truly become strong. And, they remember that it is the Lord who has called them to battle. It is the Lord who fights with and for them. They begin to know that with the presence of the Lord, they are like the mighty men of old. They are warriors who run toward the sound of battle and not away from it. Amen?

"Praise be to the Lord, for he has heard my cry for mercy. The Lord is my strength and my shield; my heart trusts in him, and I am helped. My heart leaps for joy and I will give thanks to him in song." (Psalm 28:6-7, NIV)

As we remember what He has done in the past, TRUST BUILDS. Faith grows when we remember the mighty acts of God in the past. Revelation 19:10 says, *"...Worship God! For the testimony of Jesus is the spirit of prophecy."* As we remember who Jesus is and what he has done it fills our hearts with prophetic words about what He will do. As we remember all the healing miracles, we build our faith that He can and will heal us. When we remember how He delivered people from oppressive spirits, we build our confidence that He can and will deliver us, and we begin to speak prophetic words of deliverance. The more we testify about Jesus building people up, encouraging them, and comforting them the stronger that word or prophecy becomes in us.

As we worship, we literally release the power of God in our lives. This is an advanced skill, because the normal reaction when something painful or threatening happens is panic, anxiety and fear. Without training, people want to run and hide. It is as if they will try anything but God. Someone described the situation in a little town going through hard times. One of those present at a church meeting said, "Maybe we should pray about it." Another person looked over and responded, "Has it come to that?" We know that for many people, prayer is the last resort when it should be the first response. If you can learn the advanced skill of going to God first with prayer, praise, and worship, you will change every circumstance in your life.

"What then shall we say to these things? If God is for us, who can be against us?

He who did not spare His own Son, but delivered Him up for us all, how shall He not with Him also freely give us all things? Who shall bring a charge against God's elect? It is God who justifies. Who is he who condemns? It is Christ who died, and furthermore is also risen, who is even at the right hand of God, who also makes intercession for us.

Who shall separate us from the love of Christ? Shall tribulation, or distress, or persecution, or famine, or nakedness, or peril, or sword? As it is written: "For Your sake we are killed all day long; We are accounted as sheep for the slaughter." Yet in all these things we are more than conquerors through Him who loved us. For I am persuaded that neither death nor life, nor angels nor principalities nor powers, nor things present nor things to come, nor height nor depth, nor any other created thing, shall be able to separate us from the love of God which is in Christ Jesus our Lord." (Romans 8:31-39)

We need to start confessing these things. We need to put God first, and remember that our first response is to WORSHIP!

So how do you lead the charge? You always lead with worship. Worship! Worship! Worship! How can you remember to do this? The military uses reinforcement training to lock their lessons into the soldiers' minds. They just say it over and over. The official manual for Army Training listed the outline for every class as this:

1. Tell them what you are going to tell them.
2. Tell them.
3. Tell them what you told them.

Every subject is reinforced by going over it at least three times in the classroom and then conducting the training over and over. The truth is that skills degrade with time. Some skills degrade very rapidly and must be practiced daily. So, we must continually remind people and train the most important skills over and over.

In advance training, we are learning advanced skills, and the most advanced skill I know is to release the power of God through worship. There is no power on earth or anywhere in the Universe that can stop God and those Seven Spirits of God released throughout the world.

Are you ready to lead the charge? All worship warriors report to the front of the formation and lead the charge.

PRAYER FOR WORSHIP WARRIORS

Father God, we just give you praise and worship now. Sometimes we go through hard times. All of us are dealing with situations right now. (Pause and list the positive outcomes you desire to happen with God's help in each of these situations) Lord God, we praise you in every battle we face. We recognize that it is the work of the enemy against you. We are standing with you in faith against everything the enemy can throw at us.

You are our rock! You are our salvation! You are our stronghold! You are our mighty fortress! We praise and worship you for the victory which is already established in the kingdom. Lord God, we worship you and release your power to cause the enemy to flee and cower in fear. Father God we thank you for the victory, and we praise you in advance in the glorious name of Yeshua ha Messiach! Amen and Amen!

May you be filled with courage and boldness! May you be enabled and inspired to take the battle to the enemy! May you find the boldness to run toward the battle and call to others, "Follow Me!" Then you will truly be spiritual warriors with the heart of a lion! Amen and Amen!

NOTES

LESSON 2

"RECOGNIZING THE VICTORY"

It may sound strange at first to call the ability to recognize the victory an advanced skill. To the natural mind, it seems like this should be easy to do. Most people think it is easy to look at a struggle and determine who emerges as the victor. However, it is not simple or easy. You probably know people who claim to be Christians and yet they continuously confess defeat; attributing power over their lives to a defeated foe. Listening to them, it appears that they have an endless supply of tales of the woes which have befallen them. Dear friends this should not be so! Jesus Christ won the victory on the cross, and we need to live in the power of that victory. Yet, even the greatest warriors of the past have turned victories into defeats because of their own emotional and spiritual weaknesses. David, the warrior king who wrote all those beautiful Psalms proclaiming his faith in our victorious God, once turned a great victory into an emotional and spiritual defeat for Israel.

"And Joab was told, "Behold, the king is weeping and mourning for Absalom." So the victory that day was turned into mourning for all the people. For the people heard it said that day, "The king is grieved for his son."

*And the people stole back into the city that day, as
people who are ashamed steal away when they flee in
battle. But the king covered his face, and the king cried
out with a loud voice, "O my son Absalom! O Absalom,
my son, my son!" Then Joab came into the house to the
king, and said, "Today you have disgraced all your servants who today have saved your life, the lives of your
sons and daughters, the lives of your wives and the lives
of your concubines, in that you love your enemies and
hate your friends. For you have declared today that you
regard neither princes nor servants; for today I perceive
that if Absalom had lived and all of us had died today,
then it would have pleased you well. Now therefore,
arise, go out and speak comfort to your servants. For I
swear by the Lord, if you do not go out, not one will stay
with you this night. And that will be worse for you than
all the evil that has befallen you from your youth until
now."* (2 Samuel 19:1-7)

The much smaller army of David defeated and routed the
larger army of Absalom. This rebellious and presumptuous son
of David was killed by Joab and his troops, and the rebellion
was quickly brought to an end. However, David was more concerned about the loss of His rebellious and murderous son than
the lives of all the valiant men who stood with him and fought
for him at the risk of their lives. All of his soldiers were embar-
rassed and humiliated by David's behavior. The king's actions
turned the victory into shame and mourning. A day for celebration was turned into failure by David's actions. A sulking and
mournful David let his personal problems prevent him from
recognizing the victory.

How often has the church embraced defeat in the midst of
victory? How many times have we let our emotions overrule
our hearts and minds, and failed to recognize that we have the
victory in Jesus Christ? I believe that we all need to constantly

take a refresher course on recognizing the victory. We all need to look beyond ourselves and see what God is doing. We need to look beyond ourselves and be concerned for the welfare of the entire church. How many new believers have become discouraged and disheartened by the woeful tales of defeated Christians?

This is the second lesson of your Advanced Individual Training in spiritual warfare. In the first training session, we looked at how to lead a charge. By way of a short review, I remind you of four key lessons we learned:

Lesson 1: Know your potential for the kingdom of God.
Lesson 2: Let God fight His battles! Every enemy attack is His battle.
Lesson 3: Suit up, show up, worship, and watch God win the battle.
Lesson 4: Worship is the most powerful and effective way to lead a charge

As you continue in advanced training, you need to remember and stay sharp in all of the basic skills while learning new ones. You need to have a foundation in order to build a winning strategy. You never remove the foundation as you build. Everything stands on and is built up from the foundation. Always keep in mind our foundation for spiritual warfare. Do you remember what our foundation is? It is the seven Spirits of God which Jesus sent out into all the earth.

Through the work of the seven Spirits of God, His power is just as available today as it was in the New Testament church. God's power in those seven Spirits is just as powerful today as it was when they were first sent out. They are just as strong today as they will be in the Great Tribulation and during the millennial reign of Christ. There is no diminishing of the power of the Spirit, and this power is here for us today, just as it was for the First Century Church.

While I was serving as a basic training chaplain, I conducted a weekly Bible study for the soldiers. At the time, there was a popular TV show called, "Real People!" I used the popularity of the show to make a connection with the soldiers, and named the study, "Real People!" In the classroom, I would hold up a copy of the Bible and stress that it was about real people who made mistakes, fell down, got up again, were restored, and went on to do great things for the Lord. I wanted the soldiers to understand that the God who did that for David, Peter, Thomas, and others is still the same God who would do it for them.

And, now in this advanced training, I want to stress that what God did for them He will do for you. Remember how Jesus said that His disciples will do the same things He did and even more. That means that He will do these things through you and you will do even more.

> *"Most assuredly, I say to you, he who believes in Me, the works that I do he will do also; and greater works than these he will do, because I go to My Father. And whatever you ask in My name, that I will do, that the Father may be glorified in the Son. If you ask anything in My name, I will do it."* (John 14:12-14)

The Lord did not withdraw His support and abandon you. Therefore, you must not return to bondage again to the spirit of fear. This is our faith. Faith goes beyond merely believing what He is able to do. Faith is believing that He will continue to provide for our needs. Our faith stands on a firm belief that He will continue to do for us what He did for Moses, Joshua, David, Jehoshaphat, and Hezekiah.

Do you believe this? Do you believe that you can trust Him? Do you believe the Word when it says that God does not change? Do you believe the Word when it says that Jesus is the same yesterday, today, and forever? Do you have faith that He will do it for you? If you do, then you need to confess it over and over! Confess it every day! I challenge you to make the faith statements below and speak them out loud with confidence and trust.

I believe that God does not change! What He did then, he will do for me!
I believe that God is trustworthy and true! I can always count on Him!
I believe that Jesus is the same yesterday, today and forever! He is trustworthy and true!
I'm going to trust God! I will trust Him in the good times and I will trust Him in the bad times!
Every good and perfect gift comes from God! I have faith in Him! Amen?

We learned in the previous lesson that worship is warfare. Whatever you may be going through right now, worship will bring a breakthrough! Whatever the enemy may scheme and plot against you, worship will defeat it! Don't worry about what people think! They are going to think it anyway. Stop fearing people and what they may do or say, and start using your spiritual wisdom!

Today's topic may seem a little strange at first. We're looking at the advanced skill of recognizing victory. You may be wondering if people really have difficulty recognizing victory. It may sound like a simple thing, but it really isn't. You probably know people who claim to have victory in Jesus, but constantly confess that the enemy is winning battles over them and their family. Theoretically, they are claiming the victory proclaimed in the Word of God, but in the natural they are living in defeat. They have been overcome by fear, shame, addictions, depression, despair, and illness. As you look at their personal lives, you can't really detect any victory. We need to get to the place spiritually where our confessions match the Word of God. And, we need to get the victory of Jesus working in our lives as a witness to the world. No one is attracted to weak, sick, tired, depressed and defeated people. Look at your own life and ask yourself, "Would a non-believer who sees the results of God in my life be drawn to accept Jesus? You need to live out the answer to that question.

Perhaps you remember Operation Iraqi Freedom, when our military forces went into Iraq and faced the military forces of Saddam Hussein. In just a few days, his entire military collapsed and fell into total disarray. His army either surrendered or, removing their uniforms, went into hiding. When the enemy's forces are totally routed or destroyed, the fighting phase of the operation is completed. There are other phases to follow, but the primary military operation is complete. At that point, President Bush congratulated the military forces and made the statement, "Mission Complete."

This statement was militarily correct. The enemy forces had been defeated and were in total disarray. But, the American press vindictively made fun of him for this comment. They appeared to be more interested in discrediting a president they had not chosen to support than they were concerned about the success of the U.S. military. They dishonored the men and women who had fought valiantly, and actually aided the enemy by their actions. The reaction of the press on this and many other occasions encouraged and empowered a defeated enemy. They literally snatched defeat out of the jaws of victory in order to press their political agenda.

We see the same thing in spiritual warfare. People are still fighting a battle which has already been won. They are still fighting an enemy who has already been defeated. The victory has been decisively won, but the veil of the enemy has covered their eyes. They fail to realize that the grumbling of the people encourages and empowers the enemy to continue his fight. They too are snatching defeat out of the jaws of victory.

Jesus had a different way of looking at things. He saw the victory before the battle began. Before the first shot was fired,

He saw the enemy fall like lightening. He foresaw His death on the cross as a victory rather than as a defeat. He announced, *"And I, if I am lifted up from the earth, will draw all peoples to Myself."* (John 12:32) Because He had faith in God and was certain of the outcome, He held a victory parade.

JESUS HELD A VICTORY PARADE
A WEEK BEFORE THE CROSS

"Then, as He was now drawing near the descent of the Mount of Olives, the whole multitude of the disciples began to rejoice and praise God with a loud voice for all the mighty works they had seen, saying: "'Blessed is the King who comes in the name of the Lord!' Peace in heaven and glory in the highest!" And some of the Pharisees called to Him from the crowd, "Teacher, rebuke Your disciples." But He answered and said to them, "I tell you that if these should keep silent, the stones would immediately cry out." Now as He drew near, He saw the city and wept over it, saying, "If you had known, even you, especially in this your day, the things that make for your peace! But now they are hidden from your eyes. For days will come upon you when your enemies will build an embankment around you, surround you and close you in on every side, and level you, and your children within you, to the ground; and they will not leave in you one stone upon another, because you did not know the time of your visitation." (Luke 19:37-44)

As I meditated on this passage, I began to imagine how our news media would cover this event today? I tried to image the commentators talking about it on their Sunday afternoon programs. I thought about all the jokes that would be made by the late night talk-show hosts. Just imagine all the clever punch lines about a man who would have a victory parade a week before the battle. They would put millions of dollars into paying writers and spin doctors to develop more and more clever ways of mocking this man, Jesus.

Reports would probably go out about His mental health, with questions about his stability to lead a religious movement. They would search out everyone who knew him for interviews, and limit those shown on the air to the people who ridiculed him. I could imagine them interviewing His family. I thought about some of the brothers telling how they had tried to put him away quietly, but the crowd wouldn't let them near him. I could envision the news networks sending some of their most skilled attack artist to attempt to discredit Him, because His ideas and plans were so detached from all the wisdom and knowledge of the educated elite.

You see, worldly wisdom is so inferior to God's wisdom that non-spiritual people cannot get a handle on what He is trying to do or what He is saying. God's wisdom goes far beyond our own wisdom, and most people are not wise enough to recognize it. No one on earth would have thought up a battle plan like the Lord's which proclaimed that the battle was won by dying. No human would ever have come up with the idea that the way to conquer the world is to let them beat you half to death, nail you to a cross, and leave you hanging there to die. Even the disciples, after three years of personal instruction, could not understand this plan until after it happened. However, in His infinite wisdom, God knew that this was the only way to accomplish His purpose of restoring mankind.

"However, we speak wisdom among those who are mature, yet not the wisdom of this age, nor of the rulers of this age, who are coming to nothing. But we speak the wisdom of God in a mystery, the hidden wisdom which God ordained before the ages for our glory, which none of the rulers of this age knew; for had they

known, they would not have crucified the Lord of glory."
(1 Corinthians 2:6-8)

People who make fun of other people's beliefs in things of the spirit, who make fun of those who step forward for Jesus, would make the same mistake today that the people of Jesus' time made. If they were given the chance, they would crucify the Lord of Glory again. You see it today in the media and on the talk shows. The so called "educated elite" make fun of people who have made a total commitment to serving Jesus. They accuse Christians of hate crimes simply because they believe what Jesus said. They express their feelings of wanting such people imprisoned for their crimes. Many of them speak with such hatred that you can imagine them wanting to crucify Christ and all of His followers. They have used their flawed worldly logic to distort the message of love. They have mistakenly called it hate, and responded with their own form of hatred. With all the educational resources and institutional training available to them, they are no more wise that the vengeful elitists of past history.

So, the question we need to ask is: "How do we keep from repeating their mistake? To avoid making the same mistake, we need to learn something new about God. We must learn how to recognize spiritual battles. In the world today, many people say that it is foolish to talk about spiritual battles. With a total lack of understanding about the spiritual realm, they claim that all the talk of demonic spirits is antiquated and representative of primitive cultures and primitive ideas. There are many (so called) documentary shows using the most liberal and non-believing people in higher education. They are presented as experts in theology, but are no more than merchants of doubt and disbelief. Based on their own logic and in denial of all existing evidence they form theories to confuse people about the things of God. If you speak of anything spiritual, they will go on the attack and attempt to discredit you and your ideas. In the midst of all this confusion, I advise you to hold on to the promises of the Word.

"You are of God, little children, and have overcome them, because He who is in you is greater than he who is in the world. They are of the world. Therefore they speak as of the world, and the world hears them. We are of God. He who knows God hears us; he who is not of God does not hear us. By this we know the spirit of truth and the spirit of error." (1 John 4:4-6)

Based on faith and our belief in the Word of God, we know that we are in spiritual warfare. We need the gifts of the spirit to discern the spirits and know when we are under attack. But there is more to discern than just the work of enemy spirits. We must also learn how to recognize spiritual victories. It is important to know when you have won, what you have won, and what the next mission may be. It may seem simple. But, if you look at the way people have reacted in the past in looking at warfare in the natural, you will see the mistakes they have made. As they consider the spiritual realm, where they are less wise, we know that they are prone to even greater error. We also know and understand that basic human nature has not changed. Therefore, we need advanced training to understand how to recognize spiritual victory.

We must learn to break through our own worldly wisdom because we have been educated in this same natural order. We have gone to the schools, read the books, watched the documentaries, and listened to this worldly wisdom which the scripture says is "coming to nothing." We must break away from this limited way of reasoning and become free from the fear of man. Many people are too afraid to take a stand different from the mainstream of thought in their culture. They are afraid of standing out and saying, "I'm with Jesus!" We need to fear and respect God more than man. We need to remember that the victory has already been one. Jesus won it once and for all, and because of Him, we share in that victory. Remember John's affirmation:

"You are of God, little children, and have overcome them, because He who is in you is greater than he who is in the world." (1 John 4:4)

Recognizing the victory sounds simple, but it really is an advanced skill, because, we have to break through the barriers of our worldly wisdom. We need to stand in such powerful faith and resolve that we would never dream of denying our Lord or the truth He taught. We have to break free from our bondage to the flesh, and begin to see in the spirit. Being able to see in the spiritual realm is an advanced skill, and comes to us as a definite gift of the Holy Spirit. Earnestly desire this gift.

JESUS HAD WITNESSED THE DEFEAT OF THE ENEMY

Remember when the 70 disciples (other than the twelve) came back from their mission trip to the ungodly filled with joy that they had been able to exercise authority over demonic spirits. Jesus told them of something He had personally witnessed, and this event gave Him the authority to have a victory parade before His death on the cross.

"Then the seventy returned with joy, saying, "Lord, even the demons are subject to us in Your name." And He said to them, "I saw Satan fall like lightning from heaven. Behold, I give you the authority to trample on serpents and scorpions, and over all the power of the enemy, and nothing shall by any means hurt you. Nevertheless do not rejoice in this, that the spirits are subject to you,

but rather rejoice because your names are written in heaven." (Luke 10:17-19)

Jesus saw what no one else could see. In His eternal perspective (beyond time), he saw the enemy fall from heaven at such a tremendous rate of speed that it was like a lightning bolt. We might ask, "When did that fall occur?" That fall occurred before written history. In fact, it occurred before human history.

Many people have asked me why God placed Satan in the Garden of Eden where he could cause so much havoc on human beings. That is the wrong perspective. God didn't place the serpent in the garden. He placed the garden on top of the serpent where he was to be dominated and controlled or destroyed by Adam, Eve, and their descendents.

All of Satan's authority on earth has been given to him by those who are deceived. People in the first century couldn't see the victory, because their eyes were veiled. But, Jesus saw it. He was an eye witness to the event. We see the same blindness in the response of the people who were upset at Jesus confession of having witnessed these things. They could not understand His truthful confession of being a witness to the fall of Satan. They wondered, "How can a man who is alive now have been alive back then? It doesn't fit our worldly logic!" They failed to understand His words because they didn't understand who He was. They didn't understand that He was the Lord of glory. They didn't understand that as the pre-incarnate Christ, He was the active agent of God's creation. They didn't understand that before any of us existed, Jesus was already alive and working.

Because of who He is, Jesus has the ability to recognize a defeated enemy, and He wants us to understand it as well. That's why Father God sent the Holy Spirit to guide us into all truth. But, the people who killed Christ didn't have the indwelling Holy Spirit and they were not Spirit led. It is important to understand that people's eyes were veiled when they hung Jesus on the cross. Their eyes were veiled and they mistook victory for defeat. However, Jesus' eyes were never veiled. Jesus could recognize a defeated enemy when He saw him.

I want to give another example from the war in Iraq. I like to use the war in Iraq for illustrations, because it just stands out so clearly. In this war, our own press continuously encouraged a defeated enemy. There were points in that war when the enemy (the insurgents) was so beaten down that they were ready to give up and run. In spite of enormous victories, our news media encouraged them by claiming that we were losing. The enemy was losing every battle with casualties that were 10 to 100 times as great as the allies. I remember one battle in which there were 19 US Marine casualties. First, I want to make the point that no one likes to see our soldiers lose their lives. We feel the pain and empathize with their families and friends. However, the focus was so heavily placed on these losses that the public was not well informed. There were over 2,600 enemy combatants killed or captured. No one can continue to fight for long experiencing such overwhelming losses on a continual basis. At any other point in history, this would have been hailed as a tremendous victory. But our own media turned it into a defeat. After the media repeatedly presented it to the public in this way, the American people began to lose heart, and our defeated enemies were inspired to continue a war they seemed to be winning against public opinion. The press was unable or unwilling to recognize a victory.

Jesus words about the defeat of the enemy were not really a new message. Isaiah had declared it centuries before Jesus' birth. In the passage below, Isaiah gives a lament over the fallen angel, Lucifer.

"How you are fallen from heaven, O Lucifer, son of the morning! How you are cut down to the ground, You who weakened the nations! For you have said in your

heart: 'I will ascend into heaven, I will exalt my throne above the stars of God; I will also sit on the mount of the congregation On the farthest sides of the north; I will ascend above the heights of the clouds, I will be like the Most High.' Yet you shall be brought down to Sheol, To the lowest depths of the Pit. "Those who see you will gaze at you, And consider you, saying: 'Is this the man who made the earth tremble, Who shook kingdoms, Who made the world as a wilderness And destroyed its cities, Who did not open the house of his prisoners?'" (Isaiah 14:12-17)

People tend to forget victories very quickly. In Jesus' day, they had forgotten what Isaiah said. They were looking at this enemy facing them as if he had some kind of great power, when Isaiah had already prophesied his fall. Isaiah, like Jesus, had already seen it in the spiritual realm.

Jesus saw it in the Spirit. He remembered it from when He was actually there, but Israel had already forgotten the words spoken through Isaiah. It seems to be very difficult for people to hold on to a victory. We see this same problem in our own time. We see the failure to recognize a victory in both the natural world and in the spiritual realm. People today have forgotten Jesus' declaration. They have forgotten what Isaiah said. And like the press, during the war, they encourage a defeated enemy.

Some of the captured insurgents in Iraq, later revealed that they were at the point of totally giving up. They were so devastated by the overwhelming power facing them that they just wanted to quit until they heard what was being said by the American and English people. They were so encouraged by this outcome that they rose up to fight again. And, others in neighboring countries were inspired to join them in their successful campaign against the minds and hearts of the West. The insurgents were enabled to snatch victory right out of the jaws of defeat.

In the previous lesson, we looked at the way many people keep confessing that we face a really big and powerful devil. But, we have just seen that this is completely wrong. We have a really big and powerful God, and by comparison there is a tiny little devil deceitfully trying to act like he is something great. He wants to lead us into the same kind of rebellion that got him kicked out of heaven. We need to remember his results when he tries to trick us into doing the same thing. One minute he was leading worship in the throne room thinking about how good and beautiful he was, and the next moment he was thrown out like a lightning bolt. He thought he could ascend above God and look down on him from his lofty position, and in mid thought he was traveling at light speed to an ugly destiny of lies, deception, murder, strife, hatred, and the lake of fire.

We don't want to make his mistake. There is an old saying: "misery loves company." A miserable defeated devil wants to make you miserable by deceiving you into the same fate with him. He wants you to join him in his eternal misery, but don't fall for it. Let the Holy Spirit open your eyes so that you can see the truth. There is an infinite difference between the power of Satan and the power of God. Satan has been defeated and his fate is sealed. May we stop encouraging him, building him up, and making him more than he is! May we see him for what he is — a miserable and defeated foe who is little more than a dead spirit making a lot of noise. We still have the opportunity to participate in the victory, and leave this loser behind.

HOW DO WE OPEN UP TO SEE
SPIRITUAL VICTORY?

The first skill (learned in basic training) is to continuously study your smart book. I am constantly amazed by people who claim to be "born again," but admit that they seldom read the

Bible. I hear the same thing from people who claim to be spirit filled. I even hear it from people who are in ministry. They just don't find time to read the Bible. People who have been in ministry for many years have told me that they have never read the entire Bible. When you share a prophecy and relate it to an account in the Bible they unashamedly say, "I'm sorry, but I'm not familiar with that story!" I'm always amazed by that.

Something soldiers learn in the military is that they have a SMART book; the Soldier's Manual and Readiness Training manual. A soldier must have this book, study it regularly, and have the teachings committed to memory. We need to be wise enough to do likewise. We need to study our SMART book, the Bible, regularly and commit it to heart. Everything you need is in the book, but you've got to get the book in you. Remind yourself of these lessons over and over again. Remember that in military training repetition is the key to knowing and understanding basic skills.

Children love for you to read the same story to them over and over. I believe this is one of the reasons Jesus said we need to become like little children in order to enter the kingdom of heaven. Children love repetition. The stories become familiar to them and they take comfort in the predictability of outcomes. In the story books, the good people win every time, and the bad people lose every time. This is reassuring to their young minds, and we would do well to learn from them instead of trying to break this natural desire which serves them so well.

We need to learn to love repetition in the spirit realm so that we never get tired of the stories of God. This is one of the gifts of the Holy Spirit. I never tire of the stories in the Bible. I love to read them over and over, and the Holy Spirit keeps pointing out deeper meanings as I mature and as I am ready to handle more. At one time, I experienced trouble sleeping. And, one of the reasons was that I was so excited because the next thing in my awareness would be getting into the Word. I just couldn't wait for those morning hours to come. I was like a child on Christmas Eve. I was too excited about unwrapping the gifts of the Spirit to go to sleep. I want to stay childlike in that behavior. I never want to lose that zeal for the Word of God. I love the repetition, because there are some things you just need to say every day. One of those things you need to say every day is in the book of James. I don't want a day to go by without praying my prayer based on this passage! I don't want a day to go by without remembering this verse!

> *"Therefore submit to God. Resist the devil and he will flee from you."* (James 4:7)

A fleeing enemy is a defeated enemy. If he is fleeing from you, why should you fear him? Assurance comes from the knowledge that all you have to do is submit to God and resist the devil. You don't have to get into a big fight. You don't have to get a sword and chase after him. In fact, all you have to do is resist. Any time a little doubt or tiny fear comes into my mind, I immediately pray: "Father God, I submit to you; spirit, soul and body: all that I am and all that I ever will be; all that I have and all that I ever will have I submit to you. I resist the devil and in accordance with your Word and in the mighty name of Jesus, he must flee and take all his works with him! In Jesus mighty name, Amen and Amen!" By the time I finish this little pray, whatever was against me is gone. We need this kind of repetition.

Pick some key verses for yourself and confess them over and over. Get them into your heart, so that at the first little sign of an attack, you can draw out the "sword of the Spirit which is the Word of God" and vanquish the devil. All scripture is good, but there are some which are "must have" verses. James 4:7 is one of those must have verses. Luke 10:19 is another one of those must have scriptures. Get this in your heart: "Behold, I give you the authority to trample on serpents and scorpions, and over all the power of the enemy, and nothing shall by any means hurt you."

Jesus provided us with the ultimate source of military intelligence. And, now you have access to this ultimately powerful source of military intelligence. When you are fighting in a war, one of the most important resources for you is military intelligence. You want to know the status of the enemy. You want to know all of the conditions of the battlefield. You want to know as much as you can about the enemy, his forces, and his territory. So, Jesus gave us this ultimate source of intelligence for spiritual warfare. This is another "must have" verse which should be embedded in your heart. This is Jesus speaking, and I tend to take special note when Jesus is speaking.

> *"I still have many things to say to you, but you cannot bear them now. However, when He, the Spirit of truth, has come, He will guide you into all truth; for He will not speak on His own authority, but whatever He hears He will speak; and He will tell you things to come. He will glorify Me, for He will take of what is Mine and declare it to you. All things that the Father has are Mine. Therefore I said that He will take of Mine and declare it to you."* (John 16:12-15)

Can you imagine a military commander having a source like that? Think of the value to a commander to know the whole truth about the situation. And, beyond that, the commander can know what is yet to come. He is able to know the outcome of the battle before it begins. If the commander knows what is to come, he can truly prepare for it. Take heart, because this level of intelligence is available to you.

ALL TRUTH is available to you through the Holy Spirit. Remember that we are not talking about the wisdom of this world. You already have too much of that, and you know that it is "coming to nothing."

Now catch this: The Holy Spirit will tell you the very words of God. I know this is true, because I hear it every day. He will give you prophetic visions. He will tell you heaven's perspective on your situation. He will tell you what heaven is saying today. So, it's important for you to ask for the gift of the Holy Spirit. Remember how Jesus said, *"If you then, being evil, know how to give good gifts to your children, how much more will your heavenly Father give the Holy Spirit to those who ask Him!"* (Luke 11:13, NIV) This is another important verse to store in your heart and repeat regularly. It is important for us to ask for spiritual gifts, and one of these gifts is the ability to discern in the spirit realm. I believe that in these last days as spiritual warfare intensifies, one of the most important gifts is "distinguishing between spirits."

"There are diversities of gifts, but the same Spirit. There are differences of ministries, but the same Lord. And there are diversities of activities, but it is the same God who works all in all. But the manifestation of the Spirit is given to each one for the profit of all: for to one is given the word of wisdom through the Spirit, to another the word of knowledge through the same Spirit, to another faith by the same Spirit, to another gifts of healings by the same Spirit, to another the working of miracles, to another prophecy, to another discerning of spirits, to another different kinds of tongues, to another the interpretation of tongues." (1 Corinthians 12:4-10)

Notice that nine distinct spiritual gifts are presented in this passage. Do you know how many you are allowed to ask for? The answer is: all of them. You will only receive those the Holy Spirit wants you to have, but we are told we should seek all of them. Consider I Corinthians 14:1, *"Pursue love, and desire spiritual gifts, but especially that you may prophesy."* We are instructed to desire multiple gifts. Nowhere are we told to only desire a limited number. My belief is that we should desire and ask for all of them.

I have taught numerous classes and talked with many people about spiritual gifts. During these classes and discussions, I have heard many people ask to have the ability to discern evil spirits. This is part of the gift, but it is not the highest order of discernment. The highest level of discernment is to be enabled to discern the work of the Holy Spirit. This is much more important than discerning evil. In this gifting for discernment, I believe there are three distinct skills involved in distinguishing between spirits.

Skill #1:   Discerning the work of the victorious Holy Spirit. This means to be able to discern the presence and work of the seven Spirits of God. It means that one is enabled to discern in the spiritual realms the victories God has already won, and the enemies which have already been defeated.

Skill #2:   Discerning the work of defeated demons. It is important to remember that they are defeated and only empowered by our relinquishing of authority to them. Always remember the words of Luke 10:18-19 when discerning them and their work.

Skill #3:   Acting in accordance with the discernment. If you don't put action with the discernment, the gift is wasted. So, you see that you must always turn discernment into action.

It's perfectly okay to go after all of these gifts. You will never receive gifts the Holy Spirit doesn't want you to have. However, to receive and activate those gifts, you must desire them, ask for them, and be open to receive them. Remember Paul's instructions in 1 Corinthians 14:1, *"Pursue love, and desire spiritual gifts, but especially that you may prophesy."*

Ask yourself, "Is that a suggestion or a command?" It is too strong to be a mere suggestion. I believe that this is a command with a condition attached. If you pursue love first, you will be enabled to handle more of the gifts with wisdom and prudence. Without love the gifts would be dangerous in our hands. As your love grows, more gifts become available. Paul's instructions are basically a command. Desire gifts, but first desire love and pursue it with all your heart. Then, the Holy Spirit will give what you need.

If you study chapters 12-14 of First Corinthians, follow the instructions, pursue love, and receive spiritual gifts as promised, you will become a power house for the Lord. So, go for all of them knowing that the Lord will not give you more than you need. It may be that you will need one of them today and a different one tomorrow. Pray that the Lord will give you what you need when you need it.

CAN YOU SEE IT NOW? CAN YOU SEE THE VICTORY?

I see it now. Do you? If you do, confess it aloud: "I see it now! I see the victory!" We are told in scripture that God sees the end from the beginning. Think about that! If the Holy Spirit guides you into all truth, shouldn't you be able to see the end from the beginning? Remember the promise of Jesus recorded in John 16:13, *"However, when He, the Spirit of truth, has come, He will guide you into all truth; for He will not speak on His own authority, but whatever He hears He will speak; and He will tell you things to come."* When He tells you things to come, He is telling you the end from the beginning. Like Jesus, you will be enabled to see and know the victory before the battle begins.

I think it's time for a parade; a victory celebration, because the ultimate victory is always in the "NOW!" In God's eternal timing, it is now. With the power and guidance of the Holy Spirit, you can grasp it and hold on to it in your "NOW!"

We need to stand in faith and proclaim that we will no longer empower the enemy with disparaging words about all our struggles and the things the enemy is doing to us and our families. Remember how it feels when you meet people who always go through a litany of all their troubles, all their battles, and the enemies power of them. How do you feel when you listen to all of that moaning and groaning? It is depressing, isn't it? As they tell all their struggles and hardships, confess that they are losing so much, and list all the things coming against them, they are actually building up the enemy. When people do this, they encourage and empower a defeated enemy.

Instead of confessing all of these things, we should give the enemy what he deserves. We should be rubbing it into his face that Jesus has won the victory, taken all his power and authority, and returned it all to us. We should remind him every day that he has been trampled down by the feet of Jesus. Confess aloud: "Like Jesus, I am a descendent of Eve, and my foot is on your neck!" Speak the truth of the word saying, "I can trample on snakes, I can trample on scorpions, and I have authority over all the power of the enemy!" Amen? Just keep confessing it and rubbing it into his face every time he shows up.

And then, give a shout of victory to King Jesus! Can you do that? Shout, "Hallelujah! Jesus won the victory! Hallelujah!" Give a shout of praise to King Jesus, "Hallelujah, King Jesus! Hallelujah!" There is no more time for bawling and squalling. It's time for stomping and shouting! No more falling for enemy propaganda. Stop listening to all this rubbish about the enemy's power and successes! Stop confessing his propaganda! Stop focusing on costs and losses, and get your eyes fixed on Jesus who is the author and finisher of your faith!

When you focus on Jesus, you will always see the victory. I can see the victory! How about you? If you can focus on Jesus and see the victory, then confess it! Say it aloud again: "I can see the victory!" I can see the victory and I know it is real. My Lord and Savior, Jesus Christ, is the winner and I am standing in the winner's circle with Him! How about you? Where are you standing today? Are you standing with Jesus and proclaiming His victory or are you confessing enemy propaganda? At times, I think people in the past could see it more clearly. Remember the old Hymn written by E. M. Bartlett in 1939: *"Victory in Jesus"* When you sing that old song, paying attention to the words of affirmation, it builds your faith in the victory. All of those power statements lift your spirits and inspire your faith when you sing them as your own personal confession. Sing and say words like these with conviction, and release the power of the seven Spirits of God in your life and over all the power of the enemy!

We're not going out as defeated victims confessing all our hurts and woes. We're no longer confessing the power of the enemy. We are confessing the power and victory of Jesus. When we live in this faith and go into the world to confess our Lord, Jesus Christ, who overcame sin, death, hell, and the grave for each and every one of us, we are helping to draw all people to Him. Who wants to join a group of sick, tire, weak, depressed, and broken down grumblers? No one is attracted to this. People love a winner! People want to join a victorious group of overcomers. Proclaim it aloud: "I am a victor! I am not a victim! I stand with Jesus who won the victory for me! Hallelujah!"

Remember that as soon as you accepted Jesus, you had the victory. The moment you were born again, you stepped into the winner's circle. Don't let it go! Don't trade it for some cheap lie of the devil!

The next skill you need to learn in your advanced training is how to hold on to the victory. Don't let go of the victory for anything in this world. Don't give it up for some cheap thrill of the enemy! Don't let doubt and fear steal it from you! Continue to confess: "I've got the victory, and nothing can take it away!" Say it over and over: "I've got it! Nothing can take it away!"

You are victorious, and the enemy is defeated. Believe this and act on it! Stand on your faith! As Paul taught the

Ephesians: When you have done everything to stand, then keep on standing. Never back down and give up your victory in Jesus! Amen? Remember the assurance the Lord has given to us in the first letter of John.

> *"For whatever is born of God overcomes the world. And this is the victory that has overcome the world—our faith. Who is he who overcomes the world, but he who believes that Jesus is the Son of God?* (1 John 5:4-5)

Never let go of this faith! Never again confess the power of the enemy! Claim the victory and confess it continuously! Amen?

VICTORY PRAYER

Father God, we thank you for the victory which is ours through Jesus! We thank you that we don't have to go out today and fight a big, powerful devil. You have already defeated him, bound him, stepped on his neck, and put him down. By your great work and sacrifice, You have plunged us to victory in the flow of Jesus' blood. The victory is for every one of us.

You have been so good to us. Help us to remember! May we never forget what you did for us in Jesus, and what you are doing for us now through your seven Spirits. Help us, Father God, to get these scriptures (these promises) ingrained in our minds and engraved on our hearts! Lord God, help us to stand for you, stand in faith, stand for Jesus, and never give up what you have done for us. May we always stand with Jesus, because in Him we have the victory! We thank you and praise you for this ultimate victory, in the name of Yeshua ha Messiach! Amen and Amen!

NOTES

LESSON 3

"BREAKING UP POCKETS OF RESISTANCE"

Contrary to what you have seen in many movies and on TV shows, not all enemies are quickly, easily, and totally vanquished. Not all battles are completed with clearly defined and apparent successes. Wars do not always end with cleanly established boundaries and simple answers to the problems of rebuilding what was destroyed. The same things which are true in the natural are often true in the spiritual realm. In spiritual warfare, we are told that some of the enemy forces remain in the fight and are strong enough that they must be wrestled. Not all of them can be bound or cast out by rituals of deliverance. Look closely at Paul's teaching to the Ephesian church:

"Finally, my brethren, be strong in the Lord and in the power of His might. Put on the whole armor of God, that you may be able to stand against the wiles of the devil. For we do not wrestle against flesh and blood, but against principalities, against powers, against the rulers of the darkness of this age, against spiritual hosts of wickedness in the heavenly places. Therefore take up the whole armor of God, that you may be able to

withstand in the evil day, and having done all, to stand.
(Ephesians 6:10-13)

Paul lists four types of spirits which are not quickly and easily bound and cast out. They are the enemy principalities, powers, rulers of darkness, and spiritual hosts of wickedness in heavenly places. We see some of this wrestling in the New Testament. For example, when His disciples were unable to cast out a demon, Jesus explained it by saying, "*However, this kind does not go out except by prayer and fasting.*" (Matthew 17:21) The type of demon the disciples faced required wrestling during their time of prayer and fasting. Paul makes it clear that this type of demonic spirit is still here and must be dealt with through struggling with them or wrestling them. Some things are not easy, and we have to fight to establish them.

When Jesus defeated Satan, on the cross, the most important battle in human history was over, and Jesus was the total victor. Three days later, when Jesus was raised from the dead, the last of the great enemies (sin, death, hell, and the grave) were defeated. However, there remained little pockets of resistance which were left for us to clean up after these big battles. There are still demonic spirits in the world which you are commanded to cast out. In Matthew 10:8 we read that Jesus said, "Heal the sick, cleanse the lepers, raise the dead, cast out demons. Freely you have received, freely give." In Christ we have received these things, and now it is our task to freely give them to others. So we see that there remain some strongholds of the enemy which need to be brought down. Some we can cast out and others we must wrestle. The four types of spirits we must wrestle are only to be completely vanquished when they are cast into the lake of fire after the final "white throne" judgment.

IN MAJOR BATTLES
SMALL POCKETS OF RESISTANCE ARE BYPASSED

A large army moves as quickly as possible through enemy lines. The goal is to take as much territory as possible from enemy control. Losing large amounts of territory and major portions of his military forces denies the enemy the flexibility and power to continue to operate at will. He can no longer move freely through the territory which he has lost. The military forces which have taken the territory are too strong to be countered at this time and the enemy must accept his limitations. These loses greatly restrict the movement of enemy forces. They also limit the enemy's options for choosing advantageous areas for either defensive or offensive operations.

To keep moving forcefully forward, small groups are bypassed. If the major forces stopped to finish every small place of resistance, they would greatly delay the successful conclusion of the operation. These large forces need to keep moving and cause as much damage as possible in the shortest amount of time. Therefore, the little threats are simply bypassed. The military forces will return at some later time to clean up the resistance and complete the mission. A good example of this is found in the account of Joshua's conquest of the five Amorite kings.

"And it was told Joshua, saying, "The five kings have been found hidden in the cave at Makkedah." So Joshua said, "Roll large stones against the mouth of the cave, and set men by it to guard them. And do not stay there yourselves, but pursue your enemies, and attack their rear guard. Do not allow them to enter their cities, for the Lord your God has delivered them into your hand."
(Joshua 10:17-19)

At that time, the five kings no longer posed an imminent threat. They had no command and control over their forces, because they had no means of communication available to them in the cave. They were too few in number to fight any significant battle or to pose a threat for Joshua and his army. They were basically surrounded, sealed in the cave and left unable to move until Joshua could come back and deal with them. Their supply lines were gone and they were quickly depleting all of the resources available to them. Whether kings, generals, or infantry privates those who are held captive have little or no remaining combat value.

Like the five kings, small groups of enemy forces may be left behind with only a few soldiers remaining to keep them pinned down. The few who are left to guard the resistance must ensure that no more supplies or reinforcements get through, and to wage a small war of attrition against these small enemy forces. These soldiers left behind to guard the enemy may also accept the surrender of enemy troops. We saw this during Operation Desert Storm when large numbers of enemy combatants surrendered to small numbers of allied soldiers. These pockets of resistance have little will to continue the fight. Normally their morale and strength has been completely broken down. However, they can be encouraged to rise up again and fight. We must guard against any move on our part which might encourage a defeated enemy.

In some cases, the places where pockets of resistance remain are left with no one to guard them or to hold them. This happens when the priority is to maintain the maximum concentration of forces needed to win the next phase of the battle plan. After making a thorough threat analysis, a commander may decide that these small pockets of resistance do not pose a great danger or represent an imminent threat. This is a judgment call which will only be validated in time.

AFTER THE MAJOR BATTLE, FORCES ARE SENT BACK ON CLEAN UP OPERATIONS

These small pockets of enemy combatants may have good defensive positions. A small group may hold off a larger group by limiting their access. For example the mouth of a cave limits the number of soldiers who can be engaged in battle at any given time. A small group in the cave can hold off a much larger group trying to get inside, because only three or four can fight at a time. The soldiers in the cave may also have sufficient arms and supplies to continue to fight for a long period of time. However, time is not on their side. It is only a matter of time before they fall, because slowly they are exhausting all their resources.

Fighting these small pockets of resistance can be messy. You may take additional casualties when most people believe the battle is over. These loses often seem more significant to the general public than the ones incurred in the major battle. People want to limit their losses and the end of the battle phase looks like a good time to establish these limits. So, you can see that it is easy to lose the battle for public opinion when casualties continue to be reported. When you are required to deal with these small pockets of resistance, public support for the operation may quickly erode or be lost altogether.

These small fights consume great resources. Resources of time, money, personnel, and fighting strength are expended for very little gain. After a very short time, people begin to count the cost compared to the gains. The gains are often hard to grasp and not always reported. Wars have been lost because the people have given up after counting the cost while being denied information about the gains.

People today expect instant results. On television shows and in most movies, problems are solved within 30-90 minutes. This is the expectation of many of the people. They quickly lose interest in something that goes on for a protracted time without an apparent ending point. On the other hand, people who endure long term battles with the enemy, may suffer many attacks and injures especially in the area of their physical health. Those wounded in this manner are often kept outside the view of the larger group in order to keep morale as high as possible. People do not want to be constantly confronted with suffering, and they tend to give up the battle when they reach the limit of their endurance. Jesus encountered this in His ministry when he met people who had suffered for many years. One example which really stands out is the story about the woman who had suffered the effects of a spirit of infirmity for 18 years.

"Now He was teaching in one of the synagogues on the Sabbath. And behold, there was a woman who had a spirit of infirmity eighteen years, and was bent over and could in no way raise herself up." (Luke 13:10-11)

She had been fighting this battle for eighteen years. She had wrestled it until she was ready to quit. She didn't even come to Jesus and ask to be healed. After all that warfare, she had gotten to the place of accepting her pain and suffering. She began to see and accept herself as "that woman" who was bent over from her infirmity. But this didn't fit with Jesus' plans for her. So, He initiated the healing interaction with the woman.

"But when Jesus saw her, He called her to Him and said to her, 'Woman, you are loosed from your infirmity.' And He laid His hands on her, and immediately she was made straight, and glorified God." (Luke 13:12-13)

You may be in a struggle with some of the remaining enemy forces, but it is not Jesus' desire for you to continue to battle and live with pain and suffering. He came to set you free. He came to destroy the works of the devil, and He will break that power over you. You will not be able to totally vanquish a principality, but that doesn't mean that you must resign yourself to live with the damage and limitations. You can still be set free from its power and influence, and that is Jesus' purpose and plan for your life. It is the enemy's goal to veil your eyes from the truth and persuade you to believe a lie, but you must rise above it.

Let Jesus break the power of the deception and set you free to complete you mission for the kingdom of God. The pockets of enemy forces remain, but they do not retain power over you. Remember what Jesus said in Luke 10:19, *"Behold, I give you the authority to trample on serpents and scorpions, and over all the power of the enemy, and nothing shall by any means hurt you."* You need to claim the "all" in this promise. You have authority over all of the enemy's power. You need to also claim the "nothing" in this promise. Nothing of the enemy can by any means hurt you.

We live in two realms simultaneously. We live in the natural and if we are born again, we live in the spiritual realm. Both were created by God, and both have the same basic principles. We can learn from the natural and apply the essence of the principles to the spiritual.

WHAT WE SEE IN THE NATURAL IS TRUE IN THE SPIRITUAL

Jesus fought the major battle, and Satan was defeated. Whether he recognized it or not, Satan never had a chance. The power of God is infinitely greater than all the power of Satan. We have read the book and know the ending. We win! He loses! We need to start living in that reality now. The doom of Satan and all his wicked forces is certain. There is nothing he can do about it. God knows the end from the beginning and this ending was established before the world was created. *"And He said to them, 'I saw Satan fall like lightning from heaven.'"*

(Luke 10:18) We must never lose sight of the fact that the victory belongs totally to Jesus and all those who are in Him.

As soon as it was in Satan's heart to rebel against God, he was cast out of heaven. There was no big struggle between two almost equal fighters. He was cast out and didn't even put up a fight. Remember, Satan left heaven about 1 millisecond ahead of a bolt of lightning. We know that Satan is a bad sport. If he can't have heaven, he wants to steal it from you. If he can't have life, he wants to take yours. If his work cannot last, he wants to destroy yours. His most effective tool at accomplishing his three objectives (to steal, kill, and destroy) is deception. He wants you to believe that he is still powerful. He wants you to believe that he can bless you or take the blessing from you. These are lies. Don't fall for the deception. Don't let the small remaining enemy forces persuade you to give up in defeat. Remember what Paul said to the Roman church:

> *"Yet in all these things we are more than conquerors through Him who loved us. For I am persuaded that neither death nor life, nor angels nor principalities nor powers, nor things present nor things to come, nor height nor depth, nor any other created thing, shall be able to separate us from the love of God which is in Christ Jesus our Lord."* (Romans 8:37-39)

You are more than a conqueror! You are a nation builder! As you build, you are aware that there are small pockets of resistance (little demonic forces) left behind. Do not be afraid! Do not worry! Do not give in or give up. You are more than a conqueror. There are unclean spirits left in little pockets here and there. Your mission is to do what Jesus did, and kick them out of the garden and cast them out of everyone in the garden.

> *"Now in the synagogue there was a man who had a spirit of an unclean demon. And he cried out with a loud*

voice, saying, "Let us alone! What have we to do with You, Jesus of Nazareth? Did You come to destroy us? I know who You are—the Holy One of God!" But Jesus rebuked him, saying, "And when the demon had thrown him in their midst, it came out of him and did not hurt him. Then they were all amazed and spoke among themselves, saying, "What a word this is! For with authority and power He commands the unclean spirits, and they come out." (Luke 4:33-36)

There was no big battle with these little demons. Jesus merely said with authority, "Be quiet, and come out of him!" The problem many of us have is that we don't speak with authority. We must remember that Jesus took back all the authority and then passed it on to us. We have authority over all the power of the enemy (Luke 10:19). Don't let the enemy trick you into believing a lie about his power and authority. What he wants is for you to give it back to him like Adam and Eve did in the garden. We must stop confessing the power of the devil and stand firm in confessing the power and authority of Jesus. Jesus mission statement was clearly presented to us by the apostle John:

"Little children, let no one deceive you. He who practices righteousness is righteous, just as He is righteous. He who sins is of the devil, for the devil has sinned from the beginning. For this purpose the Son of God was manifested, that He might destroy the works of the devil." (1 John 3:7-8)

John clearly states that Jesus' purpose was to "destroy the works of the devil." Do you think he failed? Absolutely not! Listen to what He declared on the cross, *"It is Finished!"* (John 19:30) Jesus declared that His part of the mission was complete.

Many ask, "So, why do we still see demons and demonic activity? Does this mean that Jesus failed?" Certainly not! These are merely the small pockets of resistance. They are very limited in power and operation. The only power they have is what you give them. Their doom is certain. They are able to do what they are doing, because people have given back their authority to the devil. We need to stay in the fight with our eyes wide open. We need to stay in the Word of God so the enemy will not be able to deceive us. We are told to test the spirits and we have been given a test to use on them. You can find it in the first chapter of First John:

"By this you know the Spirit of God: Every spirit that confesses that Jesus Christ has come in the flesh is of God, and every spirit that does not confess that Jesus Christ has come in the flesh is not of God. And this is the spirit of the Antichrist, which you have heard was coming, and is now already in the world." (1 John 4:2-3)

The spirit of the Antichrist was already operating in people during John's lifetime and it is still here today. It is not the Antichrist. It is a spirit that works through people to convince them that they do not have the victory. It tries to persuade them to disbelieve who Jesus was and who He now is. This spirit wants to convince you that your faith and walk with the Lord have all been nothing more than an illusion. Because of this strong deception, you must stay alert and continue to accomplish your purpose for the Lord. And, the Bible makes it clear that this phase of battle will not end until Jesus' returns. Does this make you want to give up easily or does it make you want to run to the sound of battle? True warriors run to the sound of battle and not away from it. Knowing your part will help you to see how these little pockets of resistance are to be handled?

THIS IS OUR AREA OF THE MISSION

The seed of Eve was and is to crush the head of the serpent. We are all descendents of Eve, and this prophetic word is for you and me. God will use your feet to crush the power of the enemy. That's why Jesus tells us to trample on the enemy forces. We are to use our feet to do the work, and it is time to do some stomping. It is time to trample on these little pockets of resistance. Every demon in your area should be terrified of you and the power in your feet. So, start stomping and don't stop.

"And He said to them, "I saw Satan fall like lightning from heaven. Behold, I give you the authority to trample on serpents and scorpions, and over all the power of the enemy, and nothing shall by any means hurt you."
(Luke 10:18-19)

We are the force to go back to the little remaining pockets of the enemy's forces and continue to do Jesus' work by destroying them. We are to "trample on serpents and scorpions," We have authority over "all the power of the enemy." Why is this so difficult for the church to grasp? We see that the church had a great struggle with this even in the New Testament times. Paul pointed out the damage the enemy had done to the church in Ephesus, and we see the same thing in the church today. We spend more time trampling each other than we spend on the enemy. Most of our churches look like the church in Paul's letter. This behavior which is a failure to follow the commands of Christ, grieves the Holy Spirit. I don't know about you, but I don't want to grieve the Holy Spirit.

"And do not grieve the Holy Spirit of God, by whom you were sealed for the day of redemption. Let all bitterness, wrath, anger, clamor, and evil speaking be put away from you, with all malice. And be kind to one another,

tenderhearted, forgiving one another, even as God in Christ forgave you." (Ephesians 4:30-32)

Why aren't we doing a better job with this mission after 1900 years? Why is the church still struggling and failing at these same points? I believe that much of it is because so many people operate with a great deal of fear. As I visit with church members, they share so many things that they fear. It is as if fear has been given free reign in the church. This should not be the way we operate. We should be operating in the power gift of faith. Faith will always overcome fear. We should be filled with the perfect love of Christ. Perfect love will cast out all our fears. If you are lacking in faith, ask God. Faith is a gift and not a work, and we know where to go to get the gift. Paul says, *"So then faith comes by hearing, and hearing by the word of God."* (Romans 10:17) Do you believe this?

If you believe that faith comes by hearing the Word of God, then I ask you where do we get all this fear? I believe that fear comes by hearing the words of the enemy. But this should not be so. We know that fear doesn't come from God. We have that assurance in the Word.

*"For God has not given us a **spirit of fear**, but of power and of love and of a sound mind."* (2 Timothy 1:7)

If you have a spirit of fear or if your spirit is controlled by fear, you can be certain that it did not come from God. God has given us many spiritual gifts, but fear is not among them. God has given you power and clear thinking, but the enemy is constantly working to cloud your thinking. It is time to set our minds free by accepting the gifts of God and rejecting the lies of the enemy. Remember that he is a liar and the father of lies. Lying is what he does for a living. Any truth you may hear from him is just a setup for a bigger lie.

The enemy has a good psychological operations plan. If he can convince you that there is an imminent danger, you will be tempted to seek self protection by holding back when you should be fighting. He has convinced some people in the church to believe that this is his time and they have no power against him. But, that is not what Jesus said. The enemy tries to overinflate his potential power and exaggerate the threat. He pretends to be as powerful as God.

"Be sober, be vigilant; because your adversary the devil walks about like a roaring lion, seeking whom he may devour. Resist him, steadfast in the faith, knowing that the same sufferings are experienced by your brotherhood in the world." (1 Peter 5:8-9)

Notice that this does not say that he is a lion. He just roars like a lion. If he can frighten people into believing he is a lion, he can use their fear to devour them. If pretending to be a big powerful threat doesn't work, he shifts his tactics, and deceives some by appearing as an angel of light.

"And no wonder! For Satan himself transforms himself into an angel of light. *Therefore it is no great thing if his ministers also transform themselves into ministers of righteousness, whose end will be according to their works."* (2 Corinthians 11:14-15)

This is why we need to test the spirits. This is why we need to know the voice of the Good Shepherd and never follow the voice of the thief and murderer, Satan. Jesus warned us about this in Matthew 24:24, *"For false christs and false prophets will rise and show great signs and wonders to deceive, if possible, even the elect."* Notice that Jesus does not say that the elect will be deceived, but he does say that the enemy will attempt it. So, we must remain alert to the enemy's propaganda messages, and only follow what we receive through the Holy Spirit.

Many fights are lost in the minds of opponents before they ever reach the field of battle. Sports teams use this trick constantly. Boxers boast greatly to frighten their opponent. Professional, seasoned fighters recognize the tactics of the enemy, and they are not intimidated by hollow claims of power and authority. Will we give up and lose the battle in our minds? We must not do this. The people of God listen to the voice of God. They know his voice and they quickly recognize a counterfeit voice. The true sheep do not listen to the voice of the thief and they do not follow him. Remember: you can recognize those who are not led by the Spirit. They do not listen to the things of God.

"You, dear children, are from God and have overcome them, because the one who is in you is greater than the one who is in the world. They are from the world and therefore speak from the viewpoint of the world, and the world listens to them." (1 John 4:4-6, NIV)

So, we come to the really big question. We must all face the challenge if we are to succeed in spiritual warfare. Here is the big question:

DO YOU HAVE THE RESOLVE TO FIGHT THE GOOD FIGHT?

Are you in it for the long haul? Many people quit at the first sign of defeat. They cannot handle a long and protracted battle. Weaker people will only continue as long as the victories are frequent and profound. But, if the progress bogs down for a short while, they are easily tempted to quit. If a few skirmishes end in a tie or if they lose a little, they are ready to throw in the towel and give up. What about you? Are you able to see the big picture and know that the victory is certain? Can you hold out no matter what it looks like in the short term? Are you committed no matter how long it takes or what it costs? Are you a committed and resilient warrior or a wimp? These are hard questions, but questions we need to face long before we go into battle. It is tragic for the other fighters when they see people quit and run.

Are you able to find ways of encouraging yourself along the way? Some use the Bible as a great source of encouragement that is always there for them regardless of what they must endure. Some walk closely with the Holy Spirit and take encouragement directly from Him. Others get linked to a group of like minded people and use the group for security. The best solution is probably a combination of all of these methods. There is strength in numbers; there is power in agreement, and there is great assurance from believing the promises of God.

Are you able to encourage others? During the build up for operation Desert Storm, a commander was briefing the soldiers on the upcoming invasion. The commander was being candid about the danger and explained what he understood of the enemy situation and capabilities. As he was giving his presentation, an officer in the back row had a panic reaction. He jumped up and shouted loudly. "We're going to die! We're all going to die!" Needless to say this had a negative impact on the morale of the soldiers. We need to realize that the things we say and do have an impact on our fellow soldiers in spiritual warfare. Are you an encourager or a discourager? Ask for God to give you supernatural boldness so that you can be a blessing to all those around you!

Are you willing to pay the price? War is costly! So many things are lost or destroyed in a war. People can lose their lives, their property, their friends, or their family members. There is a temptation to settle for peace at any cost. However this is a big mistake. The enemy's purpose will be the same whether you fight or give up. He wants to steal, kill, and destroy, and that is his plan for all of us whether we stand up or lie down. We know that when there are casualties, we can be among them. But, take heart! In Christ you have eternal life. Remember Jesus' promise, *"Jesus said to her, "I am the resurrection and the life. He who believes in Me, though he may die, he shall live. And whoever lives and believes in Me shall never die. Do you believe this?"* (John 11:25-26) Consider this important question the Lord asks of all of us, "Do you believe this?"

Many who have engaged in spiritual warfare have been seriously wounded. A reality of warfare is that there will be casualties, and it is always a very high priority to have medical treatment readily available. From the medic who travels with the war fighters to battlefield surgical centers located near the front lines these resources are needed to keep soldiers at maximum combat readiness. The absence of medical care is a serious deterrent to maintaining a high level of morale. These resources were not available to the armies of Israel during their battles. Many wounded soldiers would take their own lives rather than to allow themselves to be exposed to enemy mistreatment if they were captured in a wounded state.

"Then Saul said to his armorbearer, "Draw your sword, and thrust me through with it, lest these uncircumcised men come and abuse me." But his armorbearer would not, for he was greatly afraid. Therefore Saul took a sword and fell on it. And when his armorbearer saw that Saul was dead, he also fell on his sword and died. (1 Chronicles 10:4-5)

Spiritual war fighters may carry the scars of their wounds for many years to come. Fear of being wounded or scarred may immobilize our fighting force. Some wounded warriors withdraw in fear from spiritual warfare and become ineffective in the struggle against our ancient foes. However, the Lord promises healing for all those who are wounded by the enemy. Malachi 4:2, "*But to you who fear My name the Sun of Righteousness shall arise with healing in His wings; and you shall go out and grow fat like stall-fed calves.*" If we are going to be able to deal with the pockets of resistance remaining on the battlefield, we must be quickly healed and returned to duty. Accept your healing today and get back into the fight as soon as possible. We are all depending on one another during this cleanup phase of the battle.

To win, we must have clear goals. We must develop and hold to our initial, intermediate, and long term objectives. We cannot be deterred by the resistance we face. Resistance is to be expected, and we should not be surprised any longer that the enemy continues to attack the saints. Remember what Peter said in his first letter:

> "*Beloved, do not think it strange concerning the fiery trial which is to try you, as though some strange thing happened to you; but rejoice to the extent that you partake of Christ's sufferings, that when His glory is revealed, you may also be glad with exceeding joy. If you are reproached for the name of Christ, blessed are you, for the Spirit of glory and of God rests upon you. On their part He is blasphemed, but on your part He is glorified.*" (1 Peter 4:12-14)

To keep ourselves and others built up and strong in faith, we need to acknowledge every success. We need to celebrate and confess God's faithfulness and His constant presence to help us. Too many people in spiritual warfare are confessing the enemy's strength and successes. Every time you meet them, they have new stories about the power of the devil to attack them and do harm to them. Dear friends, we must stop encouraging and empowering the enemy and his little pockets of resistance. These confessions which attribute power and success to him are encouraging a defeated enemy. Guard your mouth! Don't let your tongue make these false confessions. Be focused and intent on giving God the honor, the power, the glory, and the praise. In every phase of the battle, you need to continue to praise the Lord for His victory. After all, you are only dealing with little pockets of resistance. The Lord is dealing with all the large, powerful enemy forces. So, praise the Lord for every victory He wins for us, and every battle which He fights so that we will not have to do it ourselves.

God gave us a great coach who can help to keep us focused and built up. It is the Holy Spirit. If you will allow Him to guide you and be totally committed to being Holy Spirit led, every battle is already won. You must learn to trust Him and respond to every order with immediate obedience. Learn now to let him build you up, encourage you, and comfort you. Remember the Lord's mission and His covenant to support you.

> *"The Spirit of the Lord God is upon Me, Because the Lord has anointed Me To preach good tidings to the poor; He has sent Me to heal the brokenhearted, To proclaim liberty to the captives, And the opening of the prison to those who are bound; To proclaim the acceptable year of the Lord, And the day of vengeance of our God; To comfort all who mourn, To console those who mourn in Zion, to give them beauty for ashes, the oil of joy for mourning, the garment of praise for the spirit of heaviness; that they may be called trees of righteousness, the planting of the LORD, that He may be glorified." (Isaiah 61:1-3)*

ADDITIONAL SCRIPTURES FOR FURTHER STUDY

ENEMY SPIRITS IN POCKETS OF RESISTANCE:

Acts 16:16 (NKJV), "Now it happened, as we went to prayer, that a certain slave girl possessed with a **spirit of divination** met us, who brought her masters much profit by fortune-telling.

Numbers 5:14 (NKJV), "...if the **spirit of jealousy** comes upon him and he becomes jealous of his wife, who has defiled herself; or if the spirit of jealousy comes upon him and he becomes jealous of his wife, although she has not defiled her-self— [Num 5:30,

Isaiah 19:3 (NKJV), "**The spirit of Egypt** will fail in its midst; I will destroy their counsel, and they will consult the idols and the charmers, the mediums and the sorcerers.

GOD'S SPIRITS SENT TO HELP US:

1 Corinthians 2:11-12 (NKJV), "For what man knows the things of a man except the spirit of the man which is in him? Even so no one knows the things of God except the Spirit of God. Now we have received, not the spirit of the world, but the Spirit who is from God, that we might know the things that have been freely given to us by God.

John 16:13 (NKJV), "However, when He, the Spirit of truth, has come, He will guide you into all truth; for He will not speak on His own *authority*, but whatever He hears He will speak; and He will tell you things to come."

2 Corinthians 4:13 (NKJV), "And since we have the same **spirit of faith**, according to what is written, *"I believed and therefore I spoke,"* we also believe and therefore speak,

WAYS OUR OWN SPIRITS MAKE US VULNERABLE:

Acts 8:20-24 (NIV), "Peter answered: "May your money perish with you, because you thought you could buy the gift of God with money! You have no part or share in this ministry, because your heart is not right before God. Repent of this wickedness and pray to the Lord. Perhaps he will forgive you for having such a thought in your heart. For I see that you are *full of bitterness* and *captive to sin*." Then Simon answered, "Pray to the Lord for me so that nothing you have said may happen to me.""

Ephesians 4:30-31 (NIV), "And do not grieve the Holy Spirit of God, with whom you were sealed for the day of redemption. Get rid of all *bitterness*, rage and anger, brawling and slander, along with every form of malice."

Hebrews 12:14-15 (NKJV), "Pursue peace with all *people*, and holiness, without which no one will see the Lord: looking carefully lest anyone fall short of the grace of God; lest any *root of bitterness* springing up cause trouble, and by this many become defiled;"

Mark 11:25 (NIV), "And when you stand praying, if you hold anything against anyone, forgive him, so that your Father in heaven may forgive you your sins."

Luke 6:37 (NIV), "Do not judge, and you will not be judged. Do not condemn, and you will not be condemned. Forgive, and you will be forgiven."

NOTES

LESSON 4

"DEVELOPING A READINESS POSTURE"

A young soldier in his second week of basic training was assigned guard duty at the ammunition storage facility. Late at night, he was fighting off a grand struggle with boredom and trying not to fall asleep on duty. He looked carefully at the area surrounding the facility and noticed a rabbit moving in the darkness. Almost instinctively he took aim and shot the rabbit. This was all very natural for him. He had grown up on a farm where hunting was a primary means of putting meat on the table. He felt very good about having hit the rabbit on the first shot. But, his celebration was cut short by the arrival of a number of Military Police vehicles filled with soldiers in full combat gear. He was arrested for discharging his weapon without cause. The charge was more serious because of the danger his actions had posed because of the ammunition stored in the facility.

We must remember who we are and who the enemy is. We are not hunting rabbits, but defending against an enemy who wants to destroy us. We are not playing games to stay awake. We are ready and watching for an enemy assault at the same time that we are getting ready to launch a counter-offensive of massive proportions. This is serious business and requires mature thinking and wise decision making. Our lives on earth and where we will spend eternity depend on our responses to the Lord.

MAINTAINING A READINESS POSTURE IS ONE OF THE MOST DIFFICULT TASKS FOR ANY ARMY

"Let your waist be girded and your lamps burning; and you yourselves be like men who wait for their master, when he will return from the wedding, that when he comes and knocks they may open to him immediately. Blessed are those servants whom the master, when he comes, will find watching. Assuredly, I say to you that he will gird himself and have them sit down to eat, and will come and serve them. And if he should come in the second watch, or come in the third watch, and find them so, blessed are those servants. But know this, that if the master of the house had known what hour the thief would come, he would have watched and not allowed his house to be broken into. Therefore you also be ready, for the Son of Man is coming at an hour you do not expect." (Luke 12:35-40)

To be obedient followers of Jesus who are prepared for the enemy's next attack, we must stay alert. However, staying alert is one of the most difficult things to teach and to learn. It takes so much energy and concentration to be constantly vigilant. When you add to this challenge the additional need to stay focused on your own mission and purpose, it is more than most people can accomplish. But, we don't give up. We rededicate ourselves to finding new and better ways to remain alert and to help others stay focused as well.

Perceiving an imminent threat is one of the best ways to stay motivated and to motivate others. In the case of our ancient enemy, we know that he never rests, he never relents, and he never backs off from his primary mission to steal, to kill, and to destroy. In basic training, someone else was responsible for keeping you alert while you were on guard duty. After you complete your training, it is your responsibility to discipline yourself. You must come to understand that it is not just your life at stake in this war. Others are depending on you when you are on watch. If you can't develop this ability to stay vigilant for yourself, do it for others you love and care about. Remember that it is an advanced skill to become one who is self disciplined and committed to helping others. We need a daily reminder of the importance of this advanced skill and it is one of our tasks to do that as well.

Paul instructed the church at Corinth, *"Watch, stand fast in the faith, be brave, be strong."* (1 Corinthians 16:13) I believe Paul had to take this action because many in the church had gone to sleep on duty. One fact known by every military leader is that soldiers fall asleep on guard duty. Therefore, the sergeant of the guard is responsible for constantly patrolling the perimeter to insure that everyone is awake and alert. This leader also makes sure that the duty is rotated every two hours. It surprises some to learn that the maximum length of time for people to stay alert is about two hours. This does not improve with training or experience. It is a part of our nature.

Jesus had the same problem. Actually it was a little worse. The disciples who were not trained as soldiers could not stay awake for one hour.

> *"Then He came and found them sleeping, and said to Peter, "Simon, are you sleeping? Could you not watch one hour? Watch and pray, lest you enter into temptation. The spirit indeed is willing, but the flesh is weak."* (Mark 14:37-38)

Almost every soldier who has ever been on guard duty can tell you the following story. "One night a very fast thinking soldier was caught sleeping by the sergeant of the guard. When his eyes opened and he saw the dilemma he was in, he quickly said, 'Amen!' The sergeant was no longer certain whether the soldier had been asleep or praying, so he did not press charges." The problem with attempting to do the same thing when you are on duty is that every sergeant of the guard has heard the same story and will not fall for it. The enemy has also heard every possible excuse and rationalization. He doesn't fall for it either. If you go to sleep on guard duty, you can count on an attack.

In the past, falling asleep on guard duty during war was punishable by death. Protecting your position, your friends, your provisions, and your leaders is too important to neglect. The Lord used this knowledge from the natural realm to teach Ezekiel a lesson he was to pass on to the people in Judah and Israel. Living in the days when enemy armies regularly roamed the land to attack unsuspecting and defenseless people, everyone knew the importance of the watchman. If the watchman was not alert or didn't sound the alarm, disaster could easily come to an entire community.

"But if the watchman sees the sword coming and does not blow the trumpet, and the people are not warned, and the sword comes and takes any person from among them, he is taken away in his iniquity; but his blood I will require at the watchman's hand.'" (Ezekiel 33:6)

Everyone is put at risk by a sleeping guard. The Lord was telling Ezekiel that the prophets were watchmen. When they received a prophetic word from the Lord, they were held accountable for sounding the alarm. This was an awesome responsibility because the people didn't want to hear the alarm. The people didn't want to know that judgment was coming. The people had even been known to kill the prophets who sounded the alarm. Nevertheless, God held the prophets responsible. Those with prophetic gifts today have the same responsibility and are held accountable by the Lord. You must decide who you are going to fear: man or God. You must decide who you want to please most: man or God.

A tragic fact is that some people are simply rebellious by nature and refuse to do their duty. We remember the story of Jonah, the unwilling prophet. In the end, he realized that he had no choice. The word of the Lord does not come back void. Knowing this, many still choose to rebel and reject the Lord's call and anointing. The Lord said to Jeremiah:

"Also, I set watchmen over you, saying, 'Listen to the sound of the trumpet!' But they said, 'We will not listen.' Therefore hear, you nations, And know, O congregation, what is among them. Hear, O earth! Behold, I will certainly bring calamity on this people— The fruit of their thoughts, Because they have not heeded My words Nor My law, but rejected it." (Jeremiah 6:17-19)

Most of us know the challenge of having to deal with rebellious people who refuse to do what they are told. We know the frustration we experience in dealing with others. Imagine the frustration for God when His people reject His word. Rebellion is a very challenging attitude to confront and correct, because the person with this attitude does not normally accept either instruction or correction. We learned this in basic training in the lesson about Korah's rebellion. When Moses was faced with rebellion, he fell face down and gave it to the Lord. Why? If you argue with a rebellious person, they become more rebellious and may become violent. If you try to defend your actions or plans with a rebellious person, you will only increase the level of animosity. Moses took the high ground through his humble response of getting face down on the ground. He didn't argue or defend himself. He left that to God. Sometimes, all we can do is pray and leave it to the work of the Holy Spirit.

Some people mean well and intend to do what they have been commanded to do, but they just can't keep their focus for very long. They intend to be faithful, vigilant and responsive, but they get distracted and lose their concentration. Others are initially rebellious, but given time, they will think it through and come to the right decision. The wise leader learns to wait and see what will develop as the Lord leads.

> *"But what do you think? A man had two sons, and he came to the first and said, 'Son, go, work today in my vineyard.' He answered and said, 'I will not,' but afterward he regretted it and went. Then he came to the second and said likewise. And he answered and said, 'I go, sir,' but he did not go. Which of the two did the will of his father?' They said to Him, 'The first.' Jesus said to them, 'Assuredly, I say to you that tax collectors and harlots enter the kingdom of God before you.'"* (Matthew 21:28-31)

The so called "righteous" people of the day looked at tax collectors and harlots as lost causes. They were viewed as sinful and rebellious, living lives in opposition to the Word of God. Yet, in Jesus day, they were responding to the gospel of the kingdom more readily than the religious leaders. The irony is that the ones claiming to be obedient were the real rebels and the ones in sin were becoming the faithful and obedient disciples. Jesus' point in this parable was that there is more hope for the rebellious son than the one who promises but does not stand by his word. The point was well made and the self-righteous leaders got the point. This is obvious from their even more rebellious reaction to Jesus.

I have often wondered how many soldiers in foxholes have promised to serve the Lord if they survived the battle, but went back on their promise when they were safe again. It is somehow part of our nature to try to bargain our way out of trouble. It is in our nature to try to defend our own rebellious behavior by presenting it in more acceptable forms. But, we must remember that we serve a covenant making God who expects faithfulness. Jesus said, *"But let your 'Yes' be 'Yes,' and your 'No,' 'No.' For whatever is more than these is from the evil one."* (Matthew 5:37) James, the brother of Jesus, took it a step further:

> *"But above all, my brethren, do not swear, either by heaven or by earth or with any other oath. But let your "Yes" be "Yes," and your "No," "No," lest you fall into judgment."* (James 5:12)

It is critically important that we do what we promise and fulfill all our vows. God takes this very seriously. In time of war, you must be able to count on the others in your unit. Your life may depend on them being where they say they will be when they say they will be there.

At my first duty station, I met an official at the bank on the installation who had retired as an Army Lieutenant Colonel. He shared his story with me. He had a very promising career and was advancing very quickly. Everyone expected him to complete a tour of duty in Vietnam with a promotion and a new job in an area of greater responsibility. However, it was all cut short when he arrived 15 seconds late for a rendezvous on the battlefield. The timing was critical, and he had been informed of the urgency. After this, he had received an evaluation report in his permanent file which labeled him as unreliable. The report recommended that he never be promoted beyond the rank of Lieutenant Colonel, and promotion boards took that comment to be worthy of consideration.

I had a difficult time understanding the importance of 15 seconds, but I took note of the need to meet all commitments. I never lost sight of this story, and made sure to always arrive on time or early for every appointment. Again, what is true in the natural is true in the spiritual. It is critically important for the Lord to know whether he can rely on you or not.

Boredom is one of the greatest enemies of readiness. We live in an age when boredom is one of the most serious maladies for our young people. Providing the tools and toys to prevent boredom is one of the major industries throughout the world. People grow up expecting to be constantly entertained. Even short periods without activity or mental input are experienced as painful. This often leads to an intense and unnatural drive for constant stimulation. For this generation, boredom results in lethargy which reduces alertness and readiness. The intense search for stimulation can divert their attention away from the mission and their readiness posture.

The reality is that people who are bored are not really paying attention. Sleep is often a desired alternative to boredom. So, taking either of these alternatives reduces your concentration and focus. A bored watchman is a danger to everyone in the city. The enemy knows our condition and takes maximum advantage from our lack of attention. Staying alert is a choice requiring dedication and vigilance at all times.

"And while they went to buy, the bridegroom came, and those who were ready went in with him to the wedding; and the door was shut. "Afterward the other virgins came also, saying, 'Lord, Lord, open to us!' But he answered and said, 'Assuredly, I say to you, I do not know you.' "Watch therefore, for you know neither the day nor the hour in which the Son of Man is coming." (Matthew 25:10-13)

As disciples of Jesus Christ we have additional reasons for staying alert. It is not just about enemy attacks. It is about the return of the master and our readiness to go into the wedding feast of the Lamb with Him. Are you ready? Have you made all the preparations? Will you be distracted by your own needs in the last hour and miss His arrival? These are all serious questions with serious consequences. You must be prepared for the arrival of either the Lord or the enemy. This requires diligence and commitment. Are you ready for it?

ENEMY FORCES DEPEND ON DECLINING VIGILANCE

All the enemy has to do is wait and watch. There is a great illustration of this in the conflict between David and Saul. Saul took the army out to find David, and as they camped overnight the entire army went to sleep. As any enemy leader might do, David took a mighty warrior with him and went near the camp to observe the enemy and found them all asleep. Listen to his chastisement of Saul's army:

> *"So David arose and came to the place where Saul had encamped. And David saw the place where Saul lay, and Abner the son of Ner, the commander of his army. Now Saul lay within the camp, with the people encamped all around him. Then David answered, and said to Ahimelech the Hittite and to Abishai the son of Zeruiah, brother of Joab, saying, "Who will go down with me to Saul in the camp?" And Abishai said, "I will go down with you."* (1 Samuel 26:5-6)

David and Abishai, one of David's mighty men, went into the camp without waking any of the sleeping soldiers. Abishai wanted to kill the king, but David would not let him. The honor David held for the anointing of the Lord was the only thing which saved Saul's life that night. David was appalled by the slack military behavior in Saul's army and severely chastised

Abner, their commander. David made it clear that because of this major military blunder Abner was deserving of death.

> *"So David said to Abner, "Are you not a man? And who is like you in Israel? Why then have you not guarded your lord the king? For one of the people came in to destroy your lord the king. This thing that you have done is not good. As the Lord lives, you deserve to die, because you have not guarded your master, the Lord's anointed. And now see where the king's spear is, and the jug of water that was by his head." (1 Samuel 26:15-16)*

As David did that night, military forces constantly probe the enemy for intelligence which will give them an advantage. A sleeping army is a very vulnerable army, and most enemy combatants will quickly take advantage of an opening in security like this.

We can be certain that our enemy operatives are well trained and highly motivated to stay focused. Anyone who infiltrates a military unit, church or corporation must remain in a high state of alertness to keep up the façade. The threat of exposure is very real and provides a strong motivation to remain alert. In time of war, spies are likely to be executed if caught. The threat of death tends to keep you focused. We know the threat which our ancient enemy poses, yet we have somehow lost the sense of urgency. We know that the enemy wants to kill us, yet we fall asleep on guard duty. We know that the enemy wants to slip in and steal our provisions, but who is watching and waiting? We know that the enemy wants to come in and destroy everything we have. So, where are the watchmen and why have they failed to give the warning?

Here is an interesting irony. The enemy is doing what the Lord told us to do. The enemy is awake, alert, and watchful. He never lets his guard down, and he is always probing our defenses to find the moment when we are all asleep. The difference here is that our enemy has no honor. Our enemy will not protect the Lord's anointed. The enemy wants to do mortal damage to every anointed servant of the Lord. Is anyone on guard duty? Is anyone watching for the enemy spies? Is anyone ready to give the alarm?

I wonder how is it that the demons are more alert than we are? Perhaps they are more clear about the reality of our warfare. Perhaps they have more to lose. Their destiny at the end of the battle is awesome and terrible, and they are motivated to hold out as long as possible. Can we do the same? What will it take to develop and maintain a state of readiness? The only answer is to increase our commitment to serve in complete surrender to the Lord and the leadership of the Holy Spirit.

Enemies continue to probe and find weaknesses in our defenses. Another thing which military organizations are trained to do is have an up to date threat analysis. One of the key components of that analysis is to know the unit's own points of weakness. It is the enemy's job to find and assault in the areas of weakness and we must be wise enough to prepare. Jesus said,

"Behold, I send you out as sheep in the midst of wolves. Therefore be wise as serpents and harmless as doves. But beware of men, for they will deliver you up to councils and scourge you in their synagogues." (Matthew 10:16-17)

Remember that in an Operations Order it is essential for you to make an estimate of friendly forces. A part of that estimate is to develop and to include a threat analysis. The threat analysis contains both the enemy's capabilities and your own vulnerabilities. As you do your own personal threat analysis, here are some key questions to address and answer:

What are your areas of weakness?
What is the point of your greatest vulnerability?
What are you doing to shore up these weaknesses?
Do you find it difficult to remain alert and ready?
How can you improve your readiness posture?

As we have learned, enemies are quick to exploit weaknesses. You will not have to wait long for an attack in an area of known weakness. The failure to remain alert and ready is a common weakness in every military force: both enemy and friendly. One of the first things the enemy will try to locate and exploit is the times when you are least ready and the guards who are least effective at maintaining security. This will be the most likely place and time of their attack. You need to be aware of these vulnerabilities well in advance and take measures to strengthen your weaknesses. There is nothing like an enemy surprise attack to wake you up and get you focused on readiness, but will it be too late?

Therefore to survive and thrive, you also must be probing your own areas of weakness. You need to examine yourself in the same way that the enemy is probing for military intelligence. As you complete this self-analysis, you need to know what to do when you find a vulnerable place in your defenses. It is great to be strong during a battle, but how much better to be so ready that the battle never happens. This has a positive and a negative effect. The positive effect is to increase your ability to prevent an attack. However, there is a negative effect. It seems that all good news has a bad news side. The bad news here is that the absence of attacks lures people into a false sense of security and they drop their defenses. Because attacks are not coming, some warriors begin to believe that they will not come again. But you must never forget the will and intent of the enemy. You can reduce the risk of invasion by shoring up your defenses, and you must also maintain a high level of readiness.

KEY: Study the Word to discover the types of weaknesses which make us most vulnerable to enemy attacks. We are each unique in our gifts, abilities, and experiences with the Lord. We have each experienced pain and loss in unique ways. Each of us needs to do an honest assessment in accordance with the Word of God. No one can tell you what you need to know in this area. It is through your relationship with the Holy Spirit and your understanding of the Word of God that you can determine the weaknesses which make you most vulnerable. Each church also needs to do an assessment based on the unique makeup of the people who are members of the congregation.

ONE OF THE 9 PRINCIPLES OF WAR IS 'SECURITY.'

"For certain men have crept in unnoticed, who long ago were marked out for this condemnation, ungodly men, who turn the grace of our God into lewdness and deny the only Lord God and our Lord Jesus Christ." (Jude 1:4)

One of the primary goals in the area of security is to keep the enemy on the outside of your camp. In the New Testament church we see that enemies have infiltrated the camp. John, Peter, Paul, and Jude all give us good examples of the issues they faced when the enemy was inside their groups. Each of these accounts adds another layer to our awareness and adds to our understanding of the problems and challenges we face. This is an ongoing process, and you are never free to get lax. If you do, you will be caught off guard and suffer the consequences.

"But there were also false prophets among the people, just as there will be false teachers among you. They will secretly introduce destructive heresies, even denying the sovereign Lord who bought them—bringing swift destruction on themselves. Many will follow their

*shameful ways and will bring the way of truth into dis-
repute. In their greed these teachers will exploit you
with stories they have made up. Their condemnation
has long been hanging over them, and their destruction
has not been sleeping."* (2 Peter 2:1-3)

Notice that false prophets and false teachers want to do their
work secretly. We will know them by the way they begin in
secret to persuade people one by one through deceitful teachings and by sharing stories which they have made up. I believe
that this will manifest through false testimonies about their
work and the way the Lord is working through them. We must
be very careful in this age to check out and verify what we are
being taught. It is very important for us to continue to seek
the gift of discerning spirits so that we cannot be deceived.
Remember the teaching of the apostle John:

*"Beloved, do not believe every spirit, but test the spirits,
whether they are of God; because many false prophets
have gone out into the world. By this you know the Spirit
of God: Every spirit that confesses that Jesus Christ has
come in the flesh is of God, and every spirit that does
not confess that Jesus Christ has come in the flesh is
not of God. And this is the spirit of the Antichrist, which
you have heard was coming, and is now already in the
world."* (1 John 4:1-3)

These false teachers and false prophets usually sound good,
because they have become expert at capturing the minds and
thoughts of those who do not know the Word. They tell exciting
stories which draw people into their webs of deceit. Be careful
of anyone who gives you a false testimony. They may have a
charismatic appeal, but they are false teachers. How do you
protect yourself against intentional falsehood? You must know
the real thing or know how to check out a teaching to validate

it in accordance with the scriptures. When the US government trains it's workers to identify counterfeit money, they do not teach them to recognize the false. They teach them to know real money so well that anything false will immediately catch their attention. We must do the same with these false teachers.

Remember Paul's praise for the believers in Berea. They had learned to stay focused on the real Word of God so that they could immediately recognize and reject the false and counterfeit. Paul proclaimed that it was honorable and fair minded to receive a teaching and then check it out in the scriptures. Notice the pattern. They received the word readily and then checked it out. You can err in either direction. If you readily receive without checking it out, you may be deceived. On the other hand, if you become unwilling to receive, you may miss out on an important teaching which will bless you. Wisdom and discernment added to willingness brings blessing.

> *"Then the brethren immediately sent Paul and Silas away by night to Berea. When they arrived, they went into the synagogue of the Jews. These were more fair-minded than those in Thessalonica, in that they received the word with all readiness, and searched the Scriptures daily to find out whether these things were so."* (Acts 17:10-11)

Knowing the Word and being Spirit led are our best defenses. These are key practices for us to develop in order to get ready and stay ready. We must learn to do this more effectively and proactively long before the enemy makes his move. We know that enemies on the inside can do serious damage. We have all been in churches, Bible study groups, and social organizations shattered by infighting. It is sad when people get emotionally hurt by the enemies in the camp. And, it is tragic when a church is split, its destiny is delayed or lost, and its members are left with permanent spiritual scars.

Notice that the false prophets and false teachers which Peter warned about make great first impressions (see 2 Peter 2:1-3). They are expert at having good appearances and using human charm to win people over and lure them into their traps. Once they have the trust of the group, they introduce subtle little variations from the truth. They don't introduce big heresies which would alarm people and cause them to doubt their man made doctrines. They are expert at using questions which lead people to doubt what they have heard before. That's what the serpent did in the garden. Remember his key question was: *"Now the serpent was more crafty than any of the wild animals the LORD God had made. He said to the woman, "Did God really say, 'You must not eat from any tree in the garden'?"* (Genesis 3:1, NIV) After he had them dealing with questions, he added something of his own and led Eve to add some of her own ideas to what God had said. Little by little Eve and Adam were led from the truth into falsehood which resulted in the fall of all mankind. This is very serious business.

False prophets and false teachers use the same tactics today to lure people away from God's truth. As Peter warns (see 2 Peter 2:1-3), they make up testimonies and tell false stories to convince you of the correctness of their teaching. Slowly they work to erode your faith and confidence in the Lord's ability to provide for us. Peter is confident of the judgment which is coming on them swiftly. That same judgment from God will come upon those who follow them and teach the same heresies.

To remain free from deception, you need to continually seek a greater anointing for the discernment of spirits. Most of all you need to improve your ability to discern the true work of the Holy Spirit. When you are operating in this gift the false and counterfeit spirits stand out and are easily recognized. In addition, you need to be able to discern enemy spirits working through those around you. Remember that you are not at war with flesh and blood. You are not called to judge people. You are called to discern and judge demonic spirits.

There is an old sports motto which states that "the best defense is a good offense." We are not called to guard the fort for the Lord. We are not asked to find a hiding place and avoid all encounters with the enemy. We are commission to trample on serpents and scorpions. We are commissioned to bring all nations to the Lord. These are not defensive operations. We need to quit waiting around for the enemy to attack. It is not enough to just know which spirit is working and how they work. We need to become proactive rather than reactive. It is time for a major offensive against the enemy and to take back all the territory on earth for the Lord. It is time to take the gospel of the kingdom to every nation on earth.

WHEN YOU'RE AT WAR
TAKE THE FIGHT TO THE ENEMY

"I have pursued my enemies and overtaken them; Neither did I turn back again till they were destroyed. I have wounded them, So that they could not rise; They have fallen under my feet. For You have armed me with strength for the battle; You have subdued under me those who rose up against me. You have also given me the necks of my enemies, so that I destroyed those who hated me. They cried out, but there was none to save; even to the Lord, but He did not answer them. Then I beat them as fine as the dust before the wind; I cast them out like dirt in the streets." (Psalm 18:37-42)

This Psalm came out of a major offensive David led against the enemies of Israel. He took the initiative and pursued the enemy until he had overtaken him and destroyed him. It is interesting that David said, *"They have fallen under my feet."* This sounds like God's charge to the seed of Eve. As he gave this testimony David is careful to give the credit to the Lord. He knew that his strength came from the Lord. He also knew that it was the Lord who had trained him and given him the battle plans. David used the strength the Lord had given him, but ultimately he knew that it was God who had truly subdued the enemy.

Taking the initiative always carries with it the element of surprise. In recent times we have called it "shock and awe." When the devastating force of a superior enemy sweeps over you, the element of surprise often leaves people in a stupor. We saw the overwhelming effect of shock and awe during in the war in Afghanistan. The Taliban did not expect the US to go on the initiative after the September 11, 2001 terrorist attacks on the World Trade Center in New York and the Pentagon. They were accustomed to acts of terror being dealt with by a relatively harmless missile shot to a remote mountaintop. They did not expect a full scale invasion, and they truly experienced "shock and awe" when it came.

The Taliban had a weakness which was quickly exploited. All of their training was for acts of terror and outmoded small scale military operations by enemies who were as poorly trained, ill equipped, and unprepared as they were. They had no tactics to deal with a full-scale invasion on their own soil. In battle after battle, they were defeated in record making short periods of time. They had no doctrine of security, had not provided proper measures to protect their borders. Air superiority immediately belonged to the invading armies, and superiority on the ground soon followed. Saddam Hussein experienced much of the same "shock and awe" because he had no strategy to deal with this type of operation. Neither Iraq nor Afghanistan expected to be invaded. Both had failed to prepared defensive positions. Neither of them had worked out a doctrine to repel enemy forces. Their command and control systems were easily disabled, and their fragmented armies dissolved into fleeing individuals.

Satan is as unprepared as the Talaban. He has been so successful with his little terror campaigns, that he has not taken the time to develop a plan to deal with the invasion which is about to come when the body of Christ discovers its true destiny and begins to follow the leadership of the Holy Spirit. In the past, the enemy has kept the Body of Christ cowering in fear by his bluffs and hollow threats. But, that time is over. Now, it is time for Joel's army to arise and take back the initiative and take the battle into his territory. Now it is time for him to experience the devastation from having an enemy inside his camp. He does not expect us to take action and he is not prepared for a full scale invasion on his own **territory.**

READINESS MUST INCLUDE BOTH DEFENSIVE AND OFFENSIVE ELEMENTS

It is not enough to merely continue to build more defensive positions. The church has been in this losing business for far too long. It is time to take territory back for the kingdom of God. It is time to bring the nations back to Father God. It is time to attack in his heart land with such ferocity that it brings shock and awe to a surprised and unprepared enemy.

Readiness has two essential meanings. First, it means being ready for an enemy attack. It means having doctrine, plans, provisions, and training to hold off the enemy for an indefinite period of time. Readiness also means to be ready to launch an offensive and invade deep inside the enemy's house. To be successful, we need strategies, training, and resources to win the big battles for the Lord. These are the things provided by the Seven Spirits of God. It is time to move on from basic training to AIT!

We need to have a heart like David when he faced Goliath. I believe this story is a foreshadowing of lines being drawn up against our ancient enemy, the devil. We must recognize that it is the Lord's battle, and we need a firm faith to believe that He will be with us and fight the battles for us. Study the battles of Jehoshaphat and Hezekiah to see how to operate with the Lord.

The Operations Order (the Bible) was written centuries ago and all the strategies have been tried and found to be highly successful.

Jesus repeatedly called on His disciples to watch and wait. *"And what I say to you, I say to all: Watch!"* (Mark 13:37)

The danger is as great today or greater than when Jesus warned the disciples. Our enemy is relentless — he will not stop until he is defeated by the Lord in the final battle at the end of time. In the meantime, stay ready! Stay Alert! Study the Word, and remember the warnings. Study the techniques and tactics of the enemy and study the methods used by the Lord. This is not the time to lose our focus and give up on our watch. Heed Peter's repeated warnings.

> "Be sober, be vigilant; because your adversary the devil walks about like a roaring lion, seeking whom he may devour. Resist him, steadfast in the faith, knowing that the same sufferings are experienced by your brotherhood in the world. But may the God of all grace, who called us to His eternal glory by Christ Jesus, after you have suffered a while, perfect, establish, strengthen, and settle *you*. To Him *be* the glory and the dominion forever and ever. Amen." (1 Peter 5:8-11)

Like David, we know the source of our strength and we know who gets the real credit for our victories. We know that without the Lord's help, we would be powerless in the days of battle. So, we place our hope and trust in the Lord, believe for the victory, and give Him all the praise and the glory. And, on our part we are vigilant, alert and watchful. Remember:

> *"Unless the Lord builds the house, they labor in vain who build it; Unless the Lord guards the city, the watchman stays awake in vain."* (Psalm 127:1)

ADDITIONAL SCRIPTURE FOR FURTHER STUDY

Matthew 24:44 (NKJV), "Therefore you also be ready, for the Son of Man is coming at an hour you do not expect."

Luke 1:17-18 (NIV), "He will also go before Him in the spirit and power of Elijah, *'to turn the hearts of the fathers to the children,'* and the disobedient to the wisdom of the just, to make ready a people prepared for the Lord."

FALSE SENSE OF READINESS:

Luke 22:31-34 (NKJV), "And the Lord said, "Simon, Simon! Indeed, Satan has asked for you, that he may sift *you* as wheat. But I have prayed for you, that your faith should not fail; and when you have returned to *Me,* strengthen your brethren." But he said to Him, "Lord, I am ready to go with You, both to prison and to death." Then He said, "I tell you, Peter, the rooster shall not crow this day before you will deny three times that you know Me.""

READINESS BASED ON FAITH IN THE LORD:

Acts 21:13 (NKJV), "Then Paul answered, "What do you mean by weeping and breaking my heart? For I am ready not only to be bound, but also to die at Jerusalem for the name of the Lord Jesus.""

2 Timothy 4:1-5 (NKJV), "I charge *you* therefore before God and the Lord Jesus Christ, who will judge the living and the dead at His appearing and His kingdom: Preach the word! Be ready in season *and* out of season. Convince, rebuke, exhort, with all longsuffering and teaching. For the time will come when they will not endure sound doctrine, but according to their own desires, *because* they have itching ears, they will heap up for themselves teachers; and they will turn *their* ears away from the truth, and be turned aside to fables. But you be watchful in all things, endure afflictions, do the work of an evangelist, fulfill your ministry."

1 Peter 3:15-16 (NKJV), "But sanctify the Lord God in your hearts, and always *be* ready to give a defense to everyone who asks you a reason for the hope that is in you, with meekness and fear; having a good conscience, that when they defame you as evildoers, those who revile your good conduct in Christ may be ashamed."

Luke 12:35-40 (NIV), "Be dressed ready for service and keep your lamps burning, like men waiting for their master to return from a wedding banquet, so that when he comes and knocks they can immediately open the door for him. It will be good for those servants whose master finds them watching when he comes. I tell you the truth, he will dress himself to serve, will have them recline at the table and will come and wait on them. It will be good for those servants whose master finds them ready, even if he comes in the second or third watch of the night. But understand this: If the owner of the house had known at what hour the thief was coming, he would not have let his house be broken into. You also must be ready, because the Son of Man will come at an hour when you do not expect him."

Luke 12:47 (NIV), "That servant who knows his master's will and does not get ready or does not do what his master wants will be beaten with many blows.

1 Corinthians 14:8 (NIV), "Again, if the trumpet does not sound a clear call, who will get ready for battle?"

1 Corinthians 16:13 (NKJV), "Watch, stand fast in the faith, be brave, be strong.

Mark 14:37-38 (NKJV), "Then He came and found them sleeping, and said to Peter, "Simon, are you sleeping? Could you not watch one hour? Watch and pray, lest you enter into temptation. The spirit indeed *is* willing, but the flesh *is* weak."

NOTES

LESSON 5

"EXERCISING SELF-CONTROL"

A young soldier was telling about his recent visit at home for the holidays. He had shocked his mother by his newly learned behavior. He got up very early, made his bed, cleaned up, dressed well, and came out to help with breakfast. He had done all of this without having to be told over and over. His mother kept thinking that he must be up to some trick to get a reward. But, she was seeing a new side of her son. Before going to basic training, he had needed a great deal of help from her and his father to maintain a disciplined lifestyle. But, in only a few weeks he was a changed man who had learned self-discipline and self-control. For the first time, he had experienced his mother and father truly being proud of him. It was a good feeling which he wanted to experience more often.

Self control must be taught. Initially, all of the controls are coming from outside sources. In the early years, it was the parents who established and maintained the controls. They worked tirelessly to teach their children well so that they could be successful in life. Then school teachers, coaches, and other authority figures added to the training by first applying the controls and then teaching the student to be self-controlled. For most young men and women, basic training takes this training to a whole new level. Every moment of every day seems to be under the control of their leaders, but gradually they are given more and more opportunities to be self controlled. The military has learned a method of training which is only complete when a soldier first learns the principles, then, watches someone else properly demonstrate the new behavior, third, practices it until it is the natural response, and then finally teaches it to another. This learning process was adopted from medical training which lists the process for learning surgical skills as: "see one, do one, and teach one."

In addition to our training and experiences in life, we have the teaching of the Bible to assist us. As Paul advised Titus, his "true son in *our* common faith," he placed a strong emphasis on spending time to teach the virtues of the Christian life in and alongside self-control. In the conduct of His ministry, Titus was to teach one generation and equip them to teach the next so that all these virtuous behaviors could be passed on to those who followed. Study closely the lesson Paul gave Titus in the following passage:

> *"You must teach what is in accord with sound doctrine. Teach the older men to be temperate, worthy of respect, self–controlled, and sound in faith, in love and in endurance. Likewise, teach the older women to be reverent in the way they live, not to be slanderers or addicted to much wine, but to teach what is good. Then they can train the younger women to love their husbands and children, to be self–controlled and pure, to be busy at home, to be kind, and to be subject to their husbands, so that no one will malign the word of God. Similarly, encourage the young men to be self–controlled."* (Titus 2:1-6, NIV)

AFTER BASIC TRAINING
SOLDIERS ARE EXPECTED TO BE
SELF-CONTROLLED

One of the teaching methods in the military is called, "BE, KNOW, DO." This basically says that if you want to "BE" a good soldier, you need to "KNOW" how to do your tasks, and then "DO" them consistently. In basic training, the lessons of self-control are taught to soldiers and many opportunities are provided to practice these skills. But, now basic training is over and it is time for the soldiers to do these things on their own, without supervision. This is what the mother saw for the first time in her son in the story at the beginning of this lesson. Being able to continue to do this over an extended period of time requires self-discipline and commitment. Old friends will work to pull you back into your old ways. Old habits are difficult to purge. You may have control over them for a time, but there is always the temptation to fall back into old patterns. Peter tells us to prepare our minds for action by three means.

> *"Therefore, prepare your minds for action; be self-controlled; set your hope fully on the grace to be given you when Jesus Christ is revealed. As obedient children, do not conform to the evil desires you had when you lived in ignorance. But just as he who called you is holy, so be holy in all you do; for it is written: "Be holy, because I am holy."* (1 Peter 1:13-16, NIV)

The first thing you need to do in getting ready for action is to be self-controlled. People who lose control easily are not effective on the battlefield. If you let your emotions rule your actions, you will not be making wise and prudent decisions. The second thing which you need is to get a clear focus on your hope for grace in the revelation of Jesus Christ. It is this hope which will supply the courage and resolve you need in the fog of war. The third thing is to purge the desires of the flesh from your mind. You have been called to holiness because God is holy.

Wise warriors prepare themselves for an attack as soon as the Spirit of holiness comes. They know from their basic training that the Spirit of holiness always attracts the spirit of rebellion. The enemy is completely predictable. He will always attempt a breach in security as you are building up for warfare. The spirit of rebellion is a very disruptive presence making readiness an even more difficult task. As you are attempting to strengthen yourself for the battle, he will send a spirit of rebellion into someone in your group who is vulnerable. In the midst of the ensuing rebellion, you will need even more self-control when you attempt to restore order. All of these situations take away precious time needed for your preparations for the battlefield.

Self-control is a difficult skill to teach. You can only know that you have self-control if and when you are placed in a situation which tempts you to lose it. This type of experiential learning is difficult to manage. Things can quickly get out of hand if someone who is armed with the weapons of war loses self-control. In addition, the measures need to test this behavioral response can easily turn into physical or emotional abuse.

However, if you can train under these circumstances and focus on self-control, you begin to build your strength. Self-control was taught experientially during Basic Training. Drill sergeants and officers were in your face all the time, seemingly daring you to lose control. Take what you learned there and keep working on it.

There is a basic human fear of losing control over your own life. You see it so clearly in elderly people who move from assisted living into a total care setting. They can no longer choose for themselves. Eventually, they are no longer able to do the simple tasks of basic self care without assistance. At this point they have basically lost all personal control over their lives. On several occasions while visiting nursing homes, I have found people trying to escape. They are not really capable of caring for themselves, but they hate losing control over their own lives. Occasionally the only means they can see for getting some control back is to escape. It is tragic to see this happening to people you care for. When I found people in this situation, I gently led them back or pushed their wheelchairs back while listening to the pain they experienced from their loss. This often helped them to resolve their pain and conflict, as least for the moment.

One of the ways to teach self-control is to put people in a position similar to confinement in nursing care units. In these settings, you can simulate the loss of self-determination and control. Military training creates this kind of environment, but to a lesser degree because of the limited duration of the training. Soldiers have very few personal options during training.

When army rangers and special operations forces train, they actually put their people through mock prisoner of war camps. The training is very realistic and the pain is very real. The cadre in these training facilities, press the pain and torture as far as possible to give people a realistic idea of how well they can handle the stress of captivity. One of these extreme training experiences takes soldiers through a mock interrogation in a simulated prisoner of war camp. To successfully pass this training, you must resist every natural instinct for self-determination. You must not lose your temper and resort to violence, fear, or panic. Many do not pass because they lose self-control.

A ranger chaplain named Dave Howard went through this training in an exemplary way. He and a group of enlisted soldiers were captured, taken to the POW camp, and interrogated with some fairly strong torture techniques. They were pushed around violently, threatened, thrown to the ground, and held down by interrogator's boots on their necks. After several unsuccessful attempts to get them to reveal secret information, the interrogators brought out some rubber hoses. They were hitting the walls and furniture with the hoses while making threats that the chaplain and his men would soon be beaten with the rubber hoses. One soldier could not take it anymore. He began to talk.

One of the interrogators knelt down over Chaplain Howard and mocked him saying, "See! We got what we wanted from this private. What are you going to do about it, now." There was a moment of silence followed by the sound of squishing mud as the chaplain struggled to get his arm free so that he could reach out and take the young soldier by the hand. Then Chaplain Howard said, "I'm going to forgive him!" That young soldier was so strengthened by the chaplain's act of compassion and grace that his resolve came back and he did not say another word. The cadre of the POW camp later said that the chaplain's act of forgiveness had completely taken them off guard. The moment he did it, they knew that they had lost the struggle. The power of forgiveness and love overcame every skill and ability these trained interrogators possessed.

A lack of self-control can easily increase behaviors arising from areas of weakness. This lack of control leaves people more vulnerable to enemy deception and demonic oppression. One of the writers of Proverbs teaches us that, *"Like a city whose walls are broken down is a man who lacks self-control."* (Proverbs 25:28, NIV) When you lose self-control, you actually break down your own defensive position. You create a hole in your own hedge of protection and leave an easy avenue of access to the enemy. When most people witness someone losing self-control, they are repulsed by the behavior. People operating in the natural realm often judge and condemn the person rather than the behavior. When a person is known to be a Christian, but has a severe loss of self-control, it results in discrediting the body of Christ. This is a tragic outcome for the cause of Christ. It is also tragic for the person who behaved this way and seriously weakened or cancelled his or her witness for Christ.

When you see someone out of control, you probable recognize it as a weakness, and that is exactly what it is. In this weakened condition, people are very much vulnerable to enemy oppression. So, what do we do about it? If we respond in anger or outwardly reject the person, we are likely to be guilty of losing our own self-control. We learn from the POW camp story that there is another alternative. We can forgive and restore people. This ends up being a very real combat multiplier. Remember that forgiving a person who has lost self-control is an advanced skill. Do you possess that skill? Unfortunately the church has a poor reputation as a source for restoration. The church is more often guilty of rejecting people who make mistakes while refusing to allow the person to be restored or reinstated. Paul made a strong case for restoration to the Galatian church.

> *"Brethren, if a man is overtaken in any trespass, you who are spiritual restore such a one in a spirit of gentleness, considering yourself lest you also be tempted. Bear one another's burdens, and so fulfill the law of Christ."* (Galatians 6:1-2)

Hopefully, we will be motivated to change when we think of the potential influence of love, forgiveness, and grace to shift the power and redeem the person and the situation.

SELF-CONTROL COMES AT A PRICE
USUALLY THROUGH HARDSHIP AND TESTING

No one likes to endure hardship while it's happening. I remember the advice I received from a seasoned veteran. He was the Sergeant Major of the Army Brigade where I was assigned. After listening to the plan for an exercise in which soldiers were to experience hardships as part of their training, He said, "You can't train soldiers to suffer. If you deprive them of water today, they will still be thirsty when you deprive them tomorrow." In one sense, he was right. Since I didn't like suffering, I sort of adopted this as a motto for a few years. Pain is the same no matter how many times you experience it. However, there is another reality at work here. You can train people to endure more pain. They will never enjoy it or get past their experience of pain, but they can learn how to cope with it and develop a new level of self-control.

Left on their own, most people will do whatever it takes to avoid pain. That's why many people don't do physical exercise regularly. It is hard, and it hurts! When our military unit was ordered to push ourselves to the point of exhaustion, the trainers would say "No pain! No gain!" I didn't really like that motto. So, I modified it to say, "No pain! No pain!" Over time as I matured and my body began to change, I realized more and more that enduring the pain today was the only way to pass the test tomorrow. This is how we learn self-control and self-discipline. We finally learn that to succeed when the battle comes, we must train constantly during the times of peace. It is difficult and it is painful, but it is also necessary.

We see the same principles at work in the spiritual realm. People tend to avoid the discipline, work, and pain it takes to get strong and stay strong in the spirit. Paul learned this lesson well during his many years on the frontlines of spiritual warfare. He had endured beatings, hardship, ship wrecks, and torture. Out of those experiences, he learned some important truths. As we study the book of Timothy, we find him handing down this wisdom and advice to his spiritual son, Timothy. We can also learn some important lessons as we study Paul's work. I like the way it was stated in "The Message."

"For bodily exercise profits a little, but godliness is profitable for all things, having promise of the life that now is and of that which is to come." (1 Timothy 4:8)

What Paul was handing down to Timothy were lessons he had learned during great tribulation and hardship. Paul paid a price to learn these lessons, and offers them to Timothy without the pain. It is wise to learn from the experiences of others so that you don't have to endure everything first hand. Paul shared with Timothy his belief that it was good to exercise and become physically strong. You need strength and endurance for the work of the ministry and the spiritual warfare which accompanies it. However, it is more essential for us to discipline ourselves and become strong and resilient in our spirits. Paul had personally gone through all these trials and continued to practice what he shared with Timothy. Unfortunately, there are not enough teachers today who practice what they preach. I can remember several teachers telling me to do what they said and not what they did. I didn't like to hear it then and I don't like to hear it now.

In Mark Chapter 8, we find Jesus giving training to the disciples and the crowds gathered around them. Many of the things Jesus taught were not readily understood because they are spirit discerned and the Holy Spirit had not yet been given. Even the disciples had difficulty understanding some of His teachings and had to ask privately for more information. One of the things which was difficult to understand is in verse 15.

"Then He charged them, saying, "Take heed, beware of the leaven of the Pharisees and the leaven of Herod." (Mark 8:15, NKJV)

You may wonder what that means. Well, the disciples wondered the same thing. Jesus knew that they were not ready to receive this teaching, so He did not elaborate until a later time. Finally, the group of believers grew in numbers and understanding to the point where they were ready to hear and understand this teaching. In Luke 12, we see that the group is now large enough to overcome the fears which had previously blocked their understanding. They were now ready to receive the teaching.

"In the meantime, when an innumerable multitude of people had gathered together, so that they trampled one another, He began to say to His disciples first of all, "Beware of the leaven of the Pharisees, which is hypocrisy." (Luke 12:1)

The leaven of the Pharisees is hypocrisy. In other words, the Pharisees were teaching others (binding others), but not personally doing what they taught. It is easy to look back and place blame on them. But the truth is that we see the same thing today. People do not always do what they say or act in accordance with what they claim to believe. Most of us reject this type of hypocrisy and pay little attention to the teaching. Knowing this, we must stay on the alert to ensure that we are not doing the same thing. Always examine yourself to see if you are practicing what you preach. If not, be aware that you are jeopardizing the effectiveness of your work.

What can you do when there are no real and effective spiritual teachers available to you? You can be self-taught. Actually, you need to go to the Word of God to learn it first hand, and then let the Holy Spirit teach you. Remember what Paul taught to the church in 1 Corinthians 2:14 (NIV), "The man without the Spirit does not accept the things that come from the Spirit of God, for they are foolishness to him, and he cannot understand them, because they are spiritually discerned." Ask the Holy Spirit to give you understanding and to teach you the deep lessons of the Word of God. This is His mission and He is faithful to carry it out. Trust Him! Ask Him for help! I have found Him to be very faithful to answer this prayer request. Jesus made this role of the Holy Spirit very clear to His disciples.

> *"I still have many things to say to you, but you cannot bear them now. However, when He, the Spirit of truth, has come, He will guide you into all truth; for He will not speak on His own authority, but whatever He hears He will speak; and He will tell you things to come."* (John 16:12-13)

With the help of the Holy Spirit, we are enabled to clearly see the needs and study to learn the solutions. After we have allowed Him to guide us into the truth, we can put it into practice. We may still need to labor hard to make positive changes, but we have powerful help in the process. It doesn't mean we will like going through this rigorous process, but we need to do it. I constantly ask for the guidance of the Holy Spirit and for Him to chasten me now so that I can be better trained and prepared for what comes next.

> *"Now no chastening seems to be joyful for the present, but painful; nevertheless, afterward it yields the peaceable fruit of righteousness to those who have been trained by it. Therefore strengthen the hands which hang down, and the feeble knees, and make straight paths for your feet, so that what is lame may not be dislocated, but rather be healed.* (Hebrews 12:11-13)

The really good news is that God is willing and able to help you. He has your best interests at heart, and whatever He does or whatever He gives is for your own good. It is done to help you to be equipped for the work of the kingdom. Many people have difficulty receiving guidance and chastening. You must see it for what it is. See it the way God sees it and it is much easier to receive. He does it because He loves you and wants you to succeed. He does it because you are His child and He wants you to recognize and know with certainty that you have been adopted into His family. His chastening proves it.

"If you endure chastening, God deals with you as with sons; for what son is there whom a father does not chasten? But if you are without chastening, of which all have become partakers, then you are illegitimate and not sons." (Hebrews 12:7-8)

Some people still reject God's teaching and training. And, you can be certain that they will reject yours as well. Don't be surprised when this happens. We have had ample warning of this possibility. Then, remember Solomon's advice:

"He who corrects a scoffer gets shame for himself, And he who rebukes a wicked man only harms himself. Do not correct a scoffer, lest he hate you; Rebuke a wise man, and he will love you. Give instruction to a wise man, and he will be still wiser; Teach a just man, and he will increase in learning." (Proverbs 9:7-9)

You must be wise enough to know who can and who cannot receive correction and instruction. If you do not make wise choices here, there is a price to pay. You will come under attack and receive abuse from those who lack the personal and emotional strength to receive correction. *"A scoffer does not love one who corrects him, Nor will he go to the wise."* (Proverbs 15:12) To assist you in developing this understanding the writer of Hebrews says:

"Furthermore, we have had human fathers who corrected us, and we paid them respect. Shall we not much more readily be in subjection to the Father of spirits and live? For they indeed for a few days chastened us as

seemed best to them, but He for our profit, that we may be partakers of His holiness." (Hebrews 12:9-10)

One day, most of you will look back and suddenly become aware that your human parents disciplined you for your own good. If you now understand that they did this for your good, how much more can you trust that God's discipline is for your own good. He does it because He wants the best to come forth from you.

LACK OF SELF CONTROL WILL HAMPER YOUR PRAYER LIFE

"The end of all things is near. Therefore be clear minded and self-controlled so that you can pray." (1 Peter 4:7, NIV)

This is an interesting quote from 1 Peter. He makes a strong connection between being clear minded and self-controlled. These two attributes go hand in hand. Peter also makes a strong tie between self-control and our ability to pray. How might the lack of self-control hamper your prayer life? After investigating this idea, I concluded that there are several ways that prayer is hindered by the lack of self-control. People without it may not be disciplined enough to maintain a consistent prayer life. Lack of consistency and regularity of communion with God tends to distance people from Him rather than drawing them closer to Him. A second reason prayers may be hinder is that people without self-control tend to jump from issue to issue without finding any resolution, and they lack the persistence to press through for answers.

A lack of self-control often manifests in a failure to manage anger. Anger which has not been placed under the control of the Holy Spirit produces bitterness and unforgiveness. You cannot bring these three character flaws into the throne room of

God. These cannot come before the throne of grace. You must forgive so that you can be forgiven. You must bless so that you can be blessed. Remember Jesus' words in Luke 4:37, *"Judge not, and you shall not be judged.* Condemn not, and you shall not be condemned. Forgive, and you will be forgiven."

> *"You have heard that it was said, 'You shall love your neighbor and hate your enemy.' But I say to you, love your enemies, bless those who curse you, do good to those who hate you, and pray for those who spitefully use you and persecute you, that you may be sons of your Father in heaven;"* (Matthew 5:43-45a)

Paul also made it plain for the church in Rome, *"Bless those who persecute you; bless and do not curse."* (Romans 12:14) If you let anger, bitterness, and unforgiveness cloud your thinking, you will not be able to serve the Lord in obedience. You will not be able to forgive and bless others as He has commanded. Without obedience, you cannot stay in union with the Lord. Jesus made it clear in John 15:10, *"If you keep My commandments, you will abide in My love, just as I have kept My Father's commandments and abide in His love."* Remaining in His love is conditional on obedience.

All these negative emotions, which are at their root disobedience to the Lord, will separate you from the Lord and you will not be effective in your prayer life. Peter says we need to be clear minded to speak with God. We must clean out our thinking and rid ourselves of all those things which separate us from God and hinder our prayers. If we are not keeping His word by loving, blessing, and forgiving, He does not abide in us. *"Jesus answered and said to him, "If anyone loves Me, he will keep My word; and My Father will love him, and We will come to him and make Our home with him."* (John 14:23) We also need to be clear minded to hear from God.

"Jesus answered them, "I told you, and you do not believe. The works that I do in My Father's name, they bear witness of Me. But you do not believe, because you are not of My sheep, as I said to you. My sheep hear My voice, and I know them, and they follow Me." (John 10:25-27)

As you rid yourself of these negative emotions, you become better able to establish and maintain a relationship with God through your prayers. This relationship with God must be based on love, respect, and blessing. These three positive attitudes open the door to the presence of the Lord. Peter gives one of the most powerful reasons why we need to love others. *"And above all things have fervent love for one another, for "love will cover a multitude of sins."* (1 Peter 4:8) Having a heart of love brings a covering over so many other things. You need to ask the Holy Spirit to help you to become filled with love as you pray.

I have observed that many people today are ultra sensitive. It often seems as if they are hyper alert and waiting for an offense. Their first reaction in almost any situation is to take offense. This character flaw is rooted in self-love, and has no place in our relationship with God. We are commanded to love others as we love ourselves. If you love others, you will not focus on their faults, failures, and sins. If you truly love others, you will not be quickly offended and respond to them in anger. People who struggle with these issues will not be effective at intercessory prayer. Their prayers will be excessively focused on their own needs with little energy being placed on praying for others. On the other hand, if you give yourself in love by loving God above all else and loving your neighbor as yourself, your prayers will be pleasing to the Lord. This kind of love wins a loving response from God.

Another important step in approaching God in prayer is to get away from all grumbling. Peter advises us to: "Be hospitable to one another without grumbling." (1 Peter 4:9) The truth is that God doesn't like grumbling or grumblers. This may shock some people who embrace a false teaching about unconditional love. God is love and He loves His entire creation, but there are certain things which will bring His wrath. Grumbling against God is one of those things which can bring judgment quickly. How much does God hate this character flaw? Listen to what He said to Moses:

> "The Lord said to Moses, "Put back Aaron's staff in front of the Testimony, to be kept as a sign to the rebellious. This will put an end to their grumbling against me, so that they will not die." (Numbers 17:10, NIV)

This is not just Old Testament theology as some have claimed. Paul told the church at Corinth, "*And do not grumble, as some of them did—and were killed by the destroying angel.*" (1 Corinthians 10:10, NIV) James also gave a similarly strong warning, "*Do not grumble against one another, brethren, lest you be condemned. Behold, the Judge is standing at the door!!*" (James 5:9) Jesus also spoke and gave a command about grumbling. "'*Stop grumbling among yourselves,' Jesus answered.*" (John 6:43) Grumblers beware: "the judge is standing at the door!" He doesn't like it when you grumble about each other and he doesn't like it when you grumble against Him. If you don't want to experience His wrath, stop grumbling.

SELF-CONTROL IS ABOUT
CONTROLLING YOURSELF

I will say it again: "Self-control is about controlling yourself!" That should go without saying, however experience shows that this is not the way it commonly works. As I speak about self-control, many people respond by thinking of other people who need to hear this. They quickly point out the behavior of others and publicly declare that they need to change. These people quickly see the lack of control in others, but are somewhat blinded to their own inability to control their emotions and behavior. So, I will say it again: "Self-control is about controlling yourself!"

> *"For if we would judge ourselves, we would not be judged. But when we are judged, we are chastened by the Lord, that we may not be condemned with the world."* (1 Corinthians 11:31-32)

Paul is saying that if we deal with ourselves now, we don't have to worry about God's judgment later. Question: Do you want to avoid being condemned? If you want to avoid condemnation, take Paul's advice and make an honest assessment of yourself. If you need help with self-control, take it to the Lord and ask for His help. Remember that the Seven Spirits of God have been sent into the world to help you overcome all these things.

Some people who quickly recognize and readily admit their lack of self-control seem to be expecting someone else to provide the controls and do the work for them. They can quickly tell you who is at fault for their behavior, but have great difficulty in admitting their own responsibility. Unless we take responsibility and seek God's help, little progress will be made. How are you doing at judging yourself? Remember how important this is for your future.

One of the challenges for many people is that their self-image is at stake. In their way of thinking, admitting to a problem makes them look bad in the eyes of others. However, a lack of self-control has already exposed them to others, and it is this behavioral response which looks very bad in the eyes of most other people. Many peace loving people will attempt to stay away from someone who easily loses control. They are unwilling to provide help for others or ask for it for themselves. Refusing help produces the opposite effect from what these people desire. Instead of protecting their reputation, they are tearing it down. They would have a much better appearance to other people and be more accepted if they admitted their problem and sought help.

"But let each one examine his own work, and then he will have rejoicing in himself alone, and not in another. For each one shall bear his own load." (Galatians 6:4-5)

This statement by Paul is not referring to the type of pride which goes before a fall. There is a healthy type of pride which assists us in being good people and doing the things which please God and other people. This kind of pride is all about conducting ourselves in a way that pleases God. When we live in a way which pleases God, it is right to feel good about it.

So many problems arise because people compare themselves with others. When they do this, they tend to hide their character flaws instead of working on them. They tend to be critical of others and try to bring them down to their own level. Jealousy is probably the most frequent outcome from comparing ourselves with others. We can all see how ugly jealous behavior is in other people around us, but we are somehow veiled to how our behavior looks to others.

Some people feel totally inadequate when compared to a highly successful person. Feelings of inadequacy tend to produce a downward spiral for the self-image of many believers. They need to get these powerful emotions under control in order to be free and blessed. To be a blessing, you need to feel blessed and favored by the Lord.

We need to take charge of our own emotions so that we can live lives that please God and bless others. People who are out of control are at risk for judgment and put others at risk for possible violence. We see this most clearly in cases of road rage. People completely lose control and behave in ways that jeopardize the safety of everyone on the road. This phenomena has led to large numbers of people being sent by judges to anger control classes. We can either deal with it ourselves or eventually someone else will. God's word tells us to take control of ourselves, and the best outcomes are always reached when we live in obedience to the Lord.

GOAL: FOR EACH TO FULLY CONTROL HIMSELF/HERSELF

"If ye love me, ye will keep my commandments. And I will pray the Father, and he shall give you another Comforter, that he may be with you for ever, even the Spirit of truth: whom the world cannot receive; for it beholdeth him not, neither knoweth him: ye know him; for he abideth with you, and shall be in you." (John 14:15-17, ASV)

Father God has not left us without help in dealing with all of our issues in this world. He has sent out the Seven Spirits of God into all the world to assist us in completing His work and doing His will. And, we can count on always receiving help from the Holy Spirit. Even though it is our task, we have the assurance of His help.

"For God has not given us a spirit of fear, but of power and of love and of a sound mind." (2 Timothy 1:7)

God did not give us a spirit of fear or timidity. He has not left us without spiritual assistance. He has sent the Holy Spirit who is a comforter and a guide. Those who operate under the anointing can expect a great deal of help and assistance from Him. Listen to just one of those promises given through the prophet Isaiah.

"The Spirit of the Lord shall rest upon Him, the Spirit of wisdom and understanding, the Spirit of counsel and might, the Spirit of knowledge and of the fear of the Lord." (Isaiah 11:2)

The Lord promises many wonderful helps for those who are Spirit led. In the Word, the number seven represents completeness. When we are told that the Lord has sent out the seven Spirits of God, we know that he means for us to have every help we need to complete our purpose and deal with the enemy. There is nothing lacking for those who receive the fullness of this outpouring of the Holy Spirit. He can restore our souls to a place of peace and self-control. He can teach us to be self-disciplined. He is a counselor, and a guide. He comes to us with gifts of wisdom, understanding, counsel, might, knowledge, and the fear of the Lord. As wonderful as it was for the disciples to have the presence of the Lord Jesus with them, He knew that they needed more, and He said:

"Nevertheless I tell you the truth. It is to your advantage that I go away; for if I do not go away, the Helper will not come to you; but if I depart, I will send Him to you." (John 16:7)

It is difficult to imagine that it would be for their good or ours for Jesus to leave the world. We would love to see Him with our own eyes, touch Him with our own hands, and to cling to him with all our might. But, this isn't what we need most. We need the Holy Spirit and all His gifts to accomplish our work and experience His protection. This doesn't mean that we will be free from enemy attacks. After the Holy Spirit came, the enemy's mission did not change. He is still trying to do the same things he has always done. He still works in your life and church to steal, kill, and destroy.

He hasn't changed, but we have. We have something now that former generations did not possess. We have the Holy Spirit abiding in us. Some people with a special anointing had the Holy Spirit on them, but we have Him in us. If we will allow Him, He will guide us, protect us, and keep us close to God. Those who are led by the Holy Spirit have fruitful lives. Look again at all the fruit of the Spirit which can be in us:

> *"But the fruit of the Spirit is love, joy, peace, longsuffering, kindness, goodness, faithfulness, gentleness, self-control. Against such there is no law."* (Galatians 5:22-23)

Those who lack self-control and are not led by the Holy Spirit also produce fruit. These are the ones who are led by the enemy and all his filthy spirits. They also produce fruit, but it is bad fruit. Their lives bring stress and hardship to themselves and everyone around them.

> *"Now the works of the flesh are evident, which are: adultery, fornication, uncleanness, lewdness, idolatry, sorcery, hatred, contentions, jealousies, outbursts of wrath, selfish ambitions, dissensions, heresies, envy, murders, drunkenness, revelries, and the like; of which I tell you beforehand, just as I also told you in time past, that those who practice such things will not inherit the kingdom of God."* (Galatians 5:19-21)

This is a very sorry list of attributes, and most of us are repelled and appalled by all of these fruits. Yet, lacking self-control, this list can easily describe us and point to the outcomes we can expect.

When we're led by the Holy Spirit, there will be good fruit in our lives, but fruit of a very different kind.. I remind you to read the Word of God aloud so that it can build your faith. Read

Galatians 5:22-23 again, and speak it out with confidence: "*But the fruit of the Spirit is love, joy, peace, longsuffering, kindness, goodness, faithfulness, gentleness, self-control. Against such there is no law.*"

You are likely in agreement that all of these are wonderful attributes. You may have also noted that Self-control was last on the list. In English, the last thing on a list is usually the least important. However, in this case the item which is listed last is in reality the key to all the others, because without it you will not be producing the other fruit in the list. I would also like for you to notice that self-control is a fruit of your relationship and obedience to the leadership of the Holy Spirit. Even self-control is not a work which we can do solely on our own. There is no works righteousness here. Even those things which we seemingly produce in our lives are still gifts from God and works of His doing.

In our lives, our churches, and our ministries, it is time to stop being surprised by the enemy. Paul reveals a strong connection between self-control and being alert and ready for the enemy. A lack of self-control may leave us in the dark where our eyes are veiled to the movement of the enemy. If we are Holy Spirit led, we are not in the dark. We see clearly and remain awake and ready.

> "*But you, brethren, are not in darkness, so that this Day should overtake you as a thief. You are all sons of light and sons of the day. We are not of the night nor of darkness. Therefore let us not sleep, as others do, but let us watch and be sober.*" (1 Thessalonians 5:4-6, NIV)

You do not belong to darkness! You do not belong to the enemy! You belong to Jesus Christ who won your freedom at a great price, and He plans for you to stay free for all eternity. You are no longer in the darkness and you do not belong to darkness. You are sons and daughters of the light and of the day. The enemy wants to steal that from you by tempting you to lose self-control. He wants to kill your dreams and destroy your destiny. So, it is time to be very alert and self-controlled. Amen?

ADDITIONAL SCRIPTURES FOR FURTHER STUDY

Titus 2:11-15 (NIV), For the grace of God that brings salvation has appeared to all men. It teaches us to say "No" to ungodliness and worldly passions, and to live self–controlled, upright and godly lives in this present age, while we wait for the blessed hope—the glorious appearing of our great God and Savior, Jesus Christ, who gave himself for us to redeem us from all wickedness and to purify for himself a people that are his very own, eager to do what is good. These, then, are the things you should teach. Encourage and rebuke with all authority. Do not let anyone despise you.

2 Timothy 3:1-5 (NKJV), "But know this, that in the last days perilous times will come: For men will be lovers of themselves, lovers of money, boasters, proud, blasphemers, disobedient to parents, unthankful, unholy, unloving, unforgiving, slanderers, without self-control, brutal, despisers of good, traitors, headstrong, haughty, lovers of pleasure rather than lovers of God, having a form of godliness but denying its power. And from such people turn away!

Titus 1:8 (NIV), "Rather he must be hospitable, one who loves what is good, who is self-controlled, upright, holy and disciplined. (this verse is about the character required of an overseer)

NOTES

LESSON 6

"WEARING PROTECTIVE EQUIPMENT"

During one tour of duty, I served as a chaplain at the Brooke Army Medical Center at Fort Sam Houston, Texas. At that time, chaplains were on the primary response team in the hospital's Level 1 Trauma Center. The primary role of the chaplain was to provide spiritual care to the patient while assisting the trauma team as liaison between the patient and the staff. Another mission was to be a liaison between family members and the medical staff. Over time another responsibility emerged. The chaplain on duty worked to protect staff members by ensuring that they were properly wearing their PPE (Personal Protective Equipment). In the rush of emergency medicine, it is easy to overlook self-care. However protection from blood-borne pathogens and exposure to serious diseases is critical for the staff to remain healthy and functional. Many times the chaplains would quietly walk over and lower the protective shield over the physicians face to provide that protection or simply hand someone a set of latex gloves.

As the senior chaplain, it was my responsibility to ensure the welfare of the other chaplains. As a result, I monitored their proper wear of the PPE. It was always surprising to find out how often this service was needed. In spite of all the classes and training, people tend to forget to use their PPE. The same thing was experienced by the soldiers in Somalia before the "Black Hawk Down" incident. Many soldiers would remove some of the Kevlar plates from their protective vests to lighten their load, but this made them vulnerable to enemy small arms fire. On that fateful day, a heavy price was paid for that small bit of convenience.

The Lord has provided His PPE for soldiers involved in spiritual warfare. Are you wearing your body armor? Do you put on the army first thing in the morning and wear it all day? Or, have you gradually slacked off during the times of relative peace? The results of failing to wear PPE are just as serious in spiritual warfare as in combat or a hospital setting. We must become proficient at using the protective equipment in order to stay fit and combat ready. Paul gives a great lesson on this in Ephesians, Chapter 6.

> "Finally, my brethren, be strong in the Lord and in the power of His might.
> Put on the whole armor of God, that you may be able to stand against the wiles of the devil. For we do not wrestle against flesh and blood, but against principalities, against powers, against the rulers of the darkness of this age, against spiritual *hosts* of wickedness in the heavenly *places*. Therefore take up the whole armor of God, that you may be able to withstand in the evil day, and having done all, to stand. Stand therefore, having girded your waist with truth, having put on the breastplate of righteousness, and having shod your feet with the preparation of the gospel of peace; above all, taking the shield of faith with which you will be able to quench all the fiery darts of the wicked one. And take the helmet of salvation, and the sword of the Spirit, which is the word of God; praying always with all prayer and sup-

plication in the Spirit, being watchful to this end with all perseverance and supplication for all the saints..." (Ephesians 6:10-18)

UNDERSTANDING THE ARMOR OF GOD

In this passage from Ephesians, Paul lists seven pieces of armor. I believe this is important because we have been given the seven Spirits of God to deal with the seven principalities of the enemy. Seven here seems to be a real number, but it also has a prophetic meaning. Seven is the number of completeness. These seven pieces of armor speak of everything you need for your protection from the works of the devil. If you need more in a particular situation or circumstance, it will be included in the seven. Lets look at these seven pieces of armor in more detail.

THE BELT OF TRUTH

In basic training, you learned that one of the principalities you must deal with is the spirit of falsehood. This spirit attempts to get you to question God's truth. It was this spirit who came against Adam and Eve in the garden. It was this spirit which deceived Israel through the work of Balaam. In His letter to the seven churches, Jesus pointed out that this same spirit was at work against them. *"But I have a few things against you, because you have there those who hold the doctrine of Balaam, who taught Balak to put a stumbling block before the children of Israel, to eat things sacrificed to idols, and to commit sexual immorality."* (Revelation 2:14). These churches were both real churches of that time, and also served as a type or example of the church in all ages.

We must still defend against the spirit of falsehood. Therefore it is critically important for us to be surrounded by the Spirit of truth: God's truth. Paul envisions this as a belt, because it must surround us to protect us from all avenues of enemy approach. In addition, as the belt, you see that every other weapon of our warfare must then hang on the belt (the truth). Without the truth of God, everything we are trying to do is futile. The first thing you need to do every morning is buckle the belt of truth around your waist! We need this in our battle against the spirit of falsehood. Jesus tells us: *"However, when He, the Spirit of truth, has come, He will guide you into all truth; for He will not speak on His own authority, but whatever He hears He will speak; and He will tell you things to come."* (John 16:13)

THE BREASTPLATE OF RIGHTEOUSNESS

The breastplate covers the heart and most of the vital organs of the body. Paul knew that the enemy always attacks the heart. If he can get into your heart, he can use you to launch additional attacks against the heart of God's people. It is the heart (the spirit of man) which is created anew when you are born again. It is created as a heart of righteousness (holiness). The enemy will send a powerful spirit against the Spirit of holiness which God has placed in your heart. He sends the spirit of rebellion (Korah) against you when you receive the Spirit of God. This is truly a heart issue. Because the enemy uses someone close to you to carry out the attack.

Balaam was an outsider, but Korah was a member of the group. It hurts deeply when someone close to you brings the attack. You are hurt by the attack, but also by the betrayal of a friend or relative. Jude mentioned the presence of this enemy activity in the church age. *"Woe to them! For they have gone in the way of Cain, have run greedily in the error of Balaam for profit, and perished in the rebellion of Korah."* (Jude 1:11) The hurt is even more intense if you lose your relationship with that person. You may actually lose that person because people can perish in their rebellion.

You must always wear the breastplate of righteousness to guard your heart. Remember Proverbs 4:23 (NIV), *"Above all else, guard your heart, for it is the wellspring of life."*

GOSPEL OF PEACE ON YOUR FEET

At first it really caught my attention when I read in Ephesians that feet should be fitted with the readiness that comes from the gospel of peace. Feet were normally considered unclean in Paul's time. It is interesting that something believed to be unclean should carry something as precious as the *"gospel of peace."* But, isn't that what the gospel is all about. God has taken us, the unclean, and fitted us to carry the gospel. Many people need to be fitted by the Lord with readiness, because readiness is difficult for us. From your study of spiritual warfare, you know that you need feet ready to respond to the Lord's command.

Feet also represent our walk with Him. This is not the only Biblical reference which makes a connection between feet and the good news. Paul wrote to the church in Rome saying, "And how shall they preach unless they are sent? As it is written: *"How beautiful are the feet of those who preach the gospel of peace, who bring glad tidings of good things!"* (Romans 10:15) Feet do not corrupt the gospel, but the gospel makes the feet beautiful and acceptable to the Lord.

When Paul made the above statement, he was making reference to two Old Testament passages. Isaiah first made this connection between feet and the good news. *"How beautiful upon the mountains are the feet of him who brings good news, who proclaims peace, who brings glad tidings of good things, who proclaims salvation, who says to Zion, "Your God reigns!"* (Isaiah 52:7) In a very similar statement, the prophet Nahum said,

"Behold, on the mountains the feet of him who brings good tidings, who proclaims peace! O Judah, keep your appointed feasts, perform your vows. For the wicked one shall no more pass through you; He is utterly cut off." (Nahum 1:15)

Are your feet ready? Have you been shod with the gospel of peace? Are you walking with the Lord and spreading the gospel of the kingdom? It is time to be taking a stand for the Lord, and standing involves your feet. Ask the Lord to put these very special shoes on your feet. Amen!

THE SHIELD OF FAITH

When I investigated this connection between faith and the shield, I was very pleasantly surprised at how many verses in the Bible make this connection. I will share three of these with you here. David proclaimed,

"The LORD is my strength and my shield; My heart trusted in Him, and I am helped; Therefore my heart greatly rejoices, and with my song I will praise Him." (Psalm 28:7)

Knowing the Lord is your shield prompts you to trust in Him and at the same time trusting in Him makes Him your shield. We see this again in a later Psalm. *"You who fear the LORD, trust in the LORD; He is their help and their shield."* (Psalm 115:11) The writer of Proverbs was wise enough to learn from the teaching of King David and later proclaimed, *"Every word of God is pure; He is a shield to those who put their trust in Him."* (Proverbs 30:5)

The shield of faith brings none other than the Lord Himself to our rescue. He guards us against every flaming arrow (word curses, accusations, false statements, and etc.) of the evil one.

You need to carry your faith (your shield) at all times. Trust in the Lord knowing that He is there to protect all those who put their faith in Him. Build up your faith by making verbal confessions of these truths. Remember, *"So then faith comes by hearing, and hearing by the word of God."* (Romans 10:17)

THE HELMET OF SALVATION

The head is the location in our bodies for the functions of our emotions, will, and reason. This is where our salvation is worked out. Paul tells the members of the Philippian church to work out their own salvation.

"Therefore, my beloved, as you have always obeyed, not as in my presence only, but now much more in my absence, work out your own salvation with fear and trembling; for it is God who works in you both to will and to do for His good pleasure." (Philippians 2:12-13)

This is not works righteousness, because it is still God who is doing the work. Our part is to cooperate in this work by letting Him bring renewal daily. As Paul said to the church in Rome:

"And do not be conformed to this world, but be transformed by the renewing of your mind, that you may prove what is that good and acceptable and perfect will of God." (Romans 12:2)

So, daily we put on the helmet of salvation to protect our souls as they are transformed by the Lord. We don't want any input or damage from the enemy. So, this area must be protected.

"But let us who are of the day be sober, putting on the breastplate of faith and love, and as a helmet the hope of salvation. For God did not appoint us to wrath, but to obtain salvation through our Lord Jesus Christ, who died for us, that whether we wake or sleep, we should live together with Him." (1 Thessalonians 5:8-10)

For soldiers on the battlefield head injuries are the most damaging. Small wounds in other parts of the body can be repaired and healed, but head injuries normally take you out of the game. I remember being on duty in the trauma center when a young husband and father of three was brought in with a head injury. This occurred on the day that the helmet law for motorcycles riders was rescinded. On his first ride without a helmet, he had an accident which left a grieving widow and three fatherless children behind. The helmet is critical. Are you wearing yours?

We know that we need this helmet, but interestingly, this is the same thing Isaiah says the Lord does,

"He saw that there was no man, and wondered that there was no intercessor; Therefore His own arm brought salvation for Him; And His own righteousness, it sustained Him. For He put on righteousness as a breastplate, and a helmet of salvation on His head; He put on the garments of vengeance for clothing, And was clad with zeal as a cloak." (Isaiah 59:16-17)

If we don't do our job, the Lord will. He will dress as we should dress, and He will show us how it should be done. I prefer to get on with the work rather than disappoint the Lord. How about you? The pieces of armor remind us again that we are made up of spirit, soul and body. The Lord provides protection in all these areas. I pray over you the prayer Paul prayed over the Thessalonians,

"Now may the God of peace Himself sanctify you completely; and may your whole spirit, soul, and body be preserved blameless at the coming of our Lord Jesus Christ." (1 Thessalonians 5:23)

THE SWORD OF THE SPIRIT

It is not enough to merely have armor to protect us during an enemy attack. We are not limited to holding down and protecting defensive positions as some have believed. We are also called to take the initiative, and carry the battle to the enemy. To do this, we need weapons, and this passage names two of them. First, we will look at the sword. Most people like to deal with the sword. It is difficult to keep people from playing with any sword which is available. As an army chaplain, I conducted many weddings, and in several the now married couple leaving the ceremony would walk under a canopy of swords held overhead by the officers in the unit. My greatest challenge was preventing sword fights during rehearsals. There is something about a sword that brings out the swashbuckler in most men and many women. So, this is usually an easy lesson to teach because the students are focused and listening when you speak of swords (especially if you have a real sword for a training aid).

Paul clarifies the meaning of the sword of the Spirit by saying that it *"is the word of God;"* (Ephesians 6:17) The Word of God is a powerful weapon. Jesus used it against Satan during the wilderness temptations. He was a much more skilled swordsman and won that battle hands down. The writer of Hebrews expands on this idea,

"For the word of God is living and powerful, and sharper than any two-edged sword, piercing even to the division of soul and spirit, and of joints and marrow, and

is a discerner of the thoughts and intents of the heart."
(Hebrews 4:12)

The word of God penetrates to the very essence of everything. It touches the delicate marrow in the bone and not just the hardened outer areas. When the Word of God is directed toward us, even the thoughts and intents of the heart are opened up to the light of the Lord where things can be fixed and resolved. When cancer strikes the bones, it works from the inside out. If the diseased bone marrow can be replaced by healthy marrow, there is a chance for healing to occur. Our greatest need for healing is deep inside us, and it is incased by a hard wall like our bones. The Holy Spirit can break through that hardness to bring restoration.

When the sword of the spirit is given to you, its purpose is more for healing your enemies than for killing them. The devil wants to kill and destroy, but God wants to heal and restore relationships. Consequently, your primary weapon is given so that you can restore broken and hostile relationships rather than doing further damage to your opponents. You need to remember how Paul started this teaching.

"For we do not wrestle against flesh and blood, but against principalities, against powers, against the rulers of the darkness of this age, against spiritual hosts of wickedness in the heavenly places." (Ephesians 6:12)

The sword is not given so that you can conduct warfare against people, but to help you cast off the demonic spirits which oppress them. The primary purpose is for people to be saved.

The Lord also has a sword and one day He will use it to kill that ancient enemy who is the serpent in the garden, the monster of the sea, and the dragon of John's revelation. We know that the outcome is certain. As Isaiah testifies,

"In that day the LORD with His severe sword, great and strong, will punish Leviathan the fleeing serpent, Leviathan that twisted serpent; and He will slay the reptile that is in the sea." (Isaiah 27:1)

You need to take up the sword of the Spirit to break off the power of the enemy from others and set them free. You do this even while you use the sword to keep yourself free from deception and enemy oppression.

PRAYING IN THE SPIRIT

The second weapon in this account is the seventh piece of the armor. It is prayer, and it is prayer of a special type. It is praying in the Spirit. This type of prayer is in a language known only to God.

"For he who speaks in a tongue does not speak to men but to God, for no one understands him; however, in the spirit he speaks mysteries." (1 Corinthians 14:2)

When you pray in this spiritual language, the enemy cannot hear what you are saying. He cannot make plans to block, counter, or counterfeit, because he has no idea what you are praying. This is primarily a type of prayer where the Holy Spirit in you prays in a spiritual language directly to God.

Paul says the you are supposed to pray like this all the time and for every kind of request. *"...praying always with all prayer and supplication in the Spirit, being watchful to this end with all perseverance and supplication for all the saints"* (Ephesians 6:18) Paul references one other way we may pray in the spirit.

"Though I speak with the tongues of men and of angels, but have not love, I have become sounding brass or a clanging cymbal." (1 Corinthians 13:1)

In this case it is the Holy Spirit praying through you with messages and directions for angels assigned to help you. This is a very powerful weapon when you are in spiritual warfare. You can use it against the enemy and at the same time for the saints. So, Paul gives this additional direction:

"And pray in the Spirit on all occasions with all kinds of prayers and requests. With this in mind, be alert and always keep on praying for all the saints." (Ephesians 6:18, NIV)

This piece of the armor is also unique because it has a defensive as well as an offensive purpose. With this piece of the armor, you can pray a canopy of protection over yourself and others who are caught up in the struggle. You can also pray to block or counter all the moves of the enemy. To be effective with this piece of the armor you need to train on both of its powerful functions: offensive and defensive. Are you using this weapon well? Ask the Holy Spirit and He will guide you into greater depths of the Spirit to become more effective.

A VISION FROM THE LORD

While writing this book, the Lord gave me a vision about this lesson. I was taken in the spirit to a vast storeroom of military equipment in heaven. The first thing I saw was battle dress uniforms in abundance to include helmets, bullet-proof vests, and other types of body armor. I saw angels picking up various items of equipment and carrying them to people who were getting prepared for spiritual warfare. As they carried items out, the supply did not diminish, and I began to sense that much more of this equipment should be distributed, but the people are not ready for it. I remembered 1 Samuel 17:

"So Saul clothed David with his armor, and he put a bronze helmet on his head; he also clothed him with a coat of mail. David fastened his sword to his armor and tried to walk, for he had not tested them. And David said to Saul, "I cannot walk with these, for I have not tested them." So David took them off." (1 Samuel 17:38-39)

David couldn't wear the armor to fight Goliath because he had not trained with it. He could not even walk while wearing the armor. Many of us are in the same condition in our spiritual warfare. We have not trained in the PPE and we do not consistently use it. When it is unfamiliar to us, it can seem awkward or cumbersome to go through the process of putting on the armor each day. As a result, we are making ourselves more and more vulnerable to an enemy attack. David had to fight Goliath without any PPE. In that fight God protected David because he was fighting the Lord's battle. After this battle things changed for David. He became a military champion and it was essential for him to be properly protected. Through frequent use, he was enabled to fight well in the armor.

However, as a man of spiritual discernment, David recognized that it was more than just his practice which had enabled him to be effective. He later testified that God had trained him and given him strength to fight in the battles which followed.

"He teaches my hands to make war, so that my arms can bend a bow of bronze. You have also given me the shield of Your salvation; Your right hand has held me up, Your gentleness has made me great. You enlarged my path under me, so my feet did not slip. I have pursued my enemies and overtaken them; Neither did I turn back again till they were destroyed." (Psalm 18:34-37)

With the training provided by the Lord and the strength which the Holy Spirit brought to him, David was enabled to fight and destroy the enemy.

In the vision I received from the Lord, I came to understand that lack of training is still an issue. Many in the body of Christ are not ready to use the equipment He provides. They are unfamiliar with it and find it difficult to wear. They lack the knowledge of what each piece of armor does to protect them and their part in using it. It is clear that we need more training in this area. At first, I thought this was a basic training subject. However, I changed my mind when I came to understand how few of us who have been in the battle for a very long time are skilled at using it. You will never become overly skilled. We all need more training and experience. And, we need to learn to put on the full armor of God daily, because we are at war with a determined and deadly enemy force each and every day. It is too late to begin your training after the battle has started.

In the vision, I looked around the storeroom in heaven to see if there were any weapons available. Since the armor had been updated from the Roman armor to today's full body armor, I wondered if the weapons of warfare were also updated. I didn't see any assault rifles, pistols, or heavy artillery. I saw a large rack containing many swords. I understood this to mean that there is nothing more modern that the "*the sword of the Spirit, which is the word of God*" (Ephesians 6:17b). The word of God is still the most powerful weapon in the Universe and you need to train with it daily. I recommend that you confess again the message from the book of Hebrews. It is a good idea to confess it often and with the strength of faith and resolve. Make it your own by making a decree in your life which is established by the Holy Spirit.

"For the word of God is living and powerful, and sharper than any two-edged sword, piercing even to the division of soul and spirit, and of joints and marrow, and

is a discerner of the thoughts and intents of the heart." (Hebrews 4:12)

The vision which the Lord gave to me came on a Tuesday morning. I heard the Lord say, "Tuesday is a training day!" In the military, Monday is not a very good training day. People are still distracted by their weekend adventures and have difficulty focusing on the tasks at hand. Many things are not ready for use on Monday, because there was no maintenance or organization of equipment over the weekend. Tuesday through Thursday are the best training days. So, today is a good day to wear the armor and train for the battle. Do it before the enemy launches another attack. Readiness is difficult to achieve, but more difficult to retain. People tend to ease up during times of peace. Then critical skills, maintenance, and resolve tend to degrade. This is the time when we need to build up a great resolve in ourselves to prepare for what lies ahead. Let's not be victims of another surprise attack by the enemy! Amen?

May the Lord train your arm for war so that you can bend a bow of bronze! May the Lord strengthen you to easily wear and wage war in the protective armor of the Spirit! May you stay ready at all times! May the Lord be with you! Amen!

THE DISCIPLINE OF WEARING PPE IS A CHALLENGE FOR ALL WARRIORS

Contrary to what you see on TV and in movies, PPE is not easy to wear. It is heavy, hot, and cumbersome. Before long, people begin to ask if the protection is worth the pain and effort. Over a period of time, people easily slip out of the discipline of wearing the PPE. It is easier and simpler to leave it off, and if the threat is not perceived to be real and imminent, this behavior begins to degrade over time. It is easier in terms of energy expended to avoid doing something than it is to actually do it.

During a tour of duty in Korea, I was the manager for the Chaplains Non-appropriated Fund. At times these duties conflicted with other military duties and accommodations had to be made. At one fund council meeting, the unit to which I was assigned was going through a drill requiring the wear of the entire set of equipment for operating in an area where chemical or biological agents had been released. The wear of the equipment for this exercise was progressive. As the threat level increased, we had to put on more and more of the equipment. Finally, we were totally covered from head to foot.

The civilians on the counsel were not participating in the exercise, but it was a challenge for them as well. The fund clerk could not recognize who made motions, gave seconds, or voted on key issues.

It was also a challenge for the military personnel. The suits were hot and uncomfortable. They limited our ability to function because it was difficult to communicate through the masks or to write with the heavy gloves. We were all happy when the exercise ended. It was the most unusual meeting we ever had, but we learned many important lessons from the exercise.

Police, soldiers, and medical personal all resist wearing PPE. It takes strong leadership to foster this behavior as the norm in a unit. However, the consequences of not being protected can be deadly. In the trauma center, it is essential to be protected; especially if the patient is infected with a life threatening disease. I was working on the team one night with a patient who had been hit by a train. The damage to his body was unimaginable. He was bleeding so profusely that the floor was about one half of an inch deep in blood. The machines could not replace his blood quickly enough so interns were squeezing bags of blood into the patient to try to keep him alive.

I was assisting a new trauma clerk to go through his personal effects to see if there was anything we needed to know for his medical care. Going through his wallet, we discovered his TB checkup card. Everyone in the room who had not properly worn the PPE had been exposed through the blood to tuberculosis. There are many pathogens which are much more deadly that this. It is a reminder of the importance of wearing PPE properly no matter how uncomfortable it may be. Dis-ease is better than disease and death. It is always essential for someone to be responsible for checking all the other team members. Are you that person? Are you checking on your family and fellow church team members to ensure that they are properly protected?

This duty of inspecting the team for readiness has traditionally fallen to the NCOs in the military. Most of them are well trained and consistent in carrying out this duty. In a medical center, this is a duty for everyone in your peer group. You must look out for one another. I believe that pastors, elders, deacons, and teachers in church should shoulder this responsibility to train and equip the saints and then to monitor their performance. Do your leaders wear their PPE and discipline the team to do the same? Responsibility always begins at the top and works down. Leaders must teach, model, monitor, and manage. Ineffective leaders produce ineffective followers.

WE ARE IN A HOSTILE ENVIRONMENT
24 HOURS A DAY

We live among germs and viruses all the time. Failure to take precautions is reckless and dangerous. We can quickly lose team members. The loss of even one team member significantly reduces our strength, readiness, and effectiveness.

We live in a world with real enemies who want to dominate and destroy us. They don't go away because we don't want to fight. In fact, this behavior (refusing to fight) which is so common today actually encourages our enemies to continue even after taking heavy losses. If we run from the battle, they will bring the battle to us. Never forget who the real enemy is and what he plans to do to you. He wants to steal your blessings, kill you, and destroy your work. That knowledge should motivate us, but over time we tend to become lax and forget. Remember: conflict is unavoidable. When your enemy declares war on you, you are at war whether you want to be or not.

In the spiritual realm, we have a real enemy, the devil. It is not a myth or an "old wives tale." Jesus was telling us the truth about this enemy and his army of fallen angels. His plans have been made clear in scripture, and whether you like it or not, he is out to kill you. He wants to devour you — to destroy you. Remember Peter's warning:

> *"Be self-controlled and alert. Your enemy the devil prowls around like a roaring lion looking for someone to devour."* (1 Peter 5:8, NIV)

As in the natural realm, we need to protect ourselves in the spiritual realm. Remember that medical personnel wear PPE, Police and soldiers wear PPE. We must also learn to put on the full armor of God.

YOU MUST TRAIN IN YOUR ARMOR
TO BE ABLE TO USE IT IN BATTLE

As you wear the armor, various parts of your body become stronger. When I first entered active duty, the helmet was made of steel and combined with the liner weighed approximately three pounds. It was a challenge to wear this helmet without constant practice. On the first day or two of wear, I would get headaches and experience intense neck pain. With the pain, I had limited movement of my head. I took that helmet off as often as possible. This was a problem for all soldiers and left us vulnerable during the times when it was not worn. Eventually, my neck would strengthen and I could wear it comfortably.

However, if a period of weeks passed without wearing it, I had to go through the entire process again.

As you serve the Lord, He will strengthen you to wear the armor. Earlier in this lesson we read of David's experience with the armor from the Psalms. These two accounts are very similar. What does it mean when God tells you something twice? The Bible includes this account twice for emphasis. So, I am including both accounts as well.

> *"He teaches my hands to make war, so that my arms can bend a bow of bronze. "You have also given me the shield of Your salvation; Your gentleness has made me great. You enlarged my path under me; So my feet did not slip. "I have pursued my enemies and destroyed them; Neither did I turn back again till they were destroyed."* (2 Samuel 22:35-38)

God made David strong enough to wear the armor and wield the weapons. When David killed Goliath, the giant's huge sword belonged to him. But, as a young man who primarily worked as a shepherd, the sword was too much for him. He was not strong enough at that time to handle the huge sword, so he left it behind. However, after God trained his arm for war, he was able to go back, take possession of the sword, and use it.

> *"And David said to Ahimelech, "Is there not here on hand a spear or a sword? For I have brought neither my sword nor my weapons with me, because the king's business required haste." So the priest said, "The sword of Goliath the Philistine, whom you killed in the Valley of Elah, there it is, wrapped in a cloth behind the ephod. If you will take that, take it. For there is no other except that one here." And David said, "There is none like it; give it to me."* (1 Samuel 21:8-9)

David had fled from Saul with such haste that he had not taken any weapons with him. This is a bad situation for a soldier. Even today, soldiers regularly do a weapons inventory. It is important to know which weapons you have on hand, and whether you have a sufficient supply to meet the needs of the battlefield. It is interesting to do a weapons inventory in the Bible.

1. **Swords**: There are at least 382 references to swords in the Bible. Some are metaphorical others are real world weapons. We have already looked at one of the real swords. In Hebrews we see the Word of God is a sword.

"For the word of God is living and powerful, and sharper than any two-edged sword, piercing even to the division of soul and spirit, and of joints and marrow, and is a discerner of the thoughts and intents of the heart." (Hebrews 4:12)

2. **Shield**: There are over 50 references to shields in the Bible. Again, some of them are real and others are metaphorical. Below you will see some of the ways shields refer to spiritual realities. These are the shields you need every day to face spiritual warfare.

"Every word of God is pure; He is a shield to those who put their trust in Him. (Proverbs 30:5)

"For the LORD God is a sun and shield; the Lord will give grace and glory; no good thing will He withhold from those who walk uprightly." (Psalm 84:11)

"You are my hiding place and my shield; I hope in Your word." (Psalm 119:114)

"After these things the word of the LORD came to Abram in a vision, saying, "Do not be afraid, Abram. I am your shield, your exceedingly great reward." (Genesis 15:1)

3. **Spear**: There are at least 43 references to spears in the Bible. Most are references to real spears, but a few are metaphorical. The enemy used a spear in the hands of a Roman soldier to pierce the Lord on the cross.

"But one of the soldiers pierced His side with a spear, and immediately blood and water came out." (John 19:34)

"Also draw out the spear, and stop those who pursue me. Say to my soul, 'I am your salvation.'" (Psalm 35:3)

"The sun and moon stood still in their habitation; at the light of Your arrows they went, at the shining of Your glittering spear. (Habakkuk 3:11)

The best armor available during the lifetime of Paul was that of the Roman legions. So, he used it to illustrate spiritual truths. By today's standards, that armor is woefully outdated. There were many places of vulnerability in the armor of that time which have been resolved over the years. I think it is time to consider an armor upgrade. Today, soldiers can have full body armor, leaving very little of the body exposed. The Kevlar will stop the bullets from small arms fire as well as shrapnel from smaller explosive devices. It is lighter, stronger, and gives better coverage of vital body parts. When you put on your armor consider full body armor.

REMEMBER: THE ENEMY HAS ARMOR TOO:

"And a champion went out from the camp of the Philistines, named Goliath, from Gath, whose height was six cubits and a span. He had a bronze helmet on his head, and he was armed with a coat of mail, and the weight of the coat was five thousand shekels of bronze. And he had bronze armor on his legs and a bronze javelin between his shoulders. Now the staff of his spear was like a weaver's beam, and his iron spearhead weighed six hundred shekels; and a shield-bearer went before him." (1 Samuel 17:4-7)

In the Bible, Goliath is a type for Satan. When he came out to do battle he was well armed and well armored. His armor seemed awesome to the army of Israel and those who wrote the Biblical accounts pointed out in great detail how he was dressed.

The enemy counterfeits everything of God, including armor and weapons. Paul points out that he will have "all kinds of counterfeit" items to deceive the saints.

"The coming of the lawless one is according to the working of Satan, with all power, signs, and lying wonders, and with all unrighteous deception among those who perish, because they did not receive the love of the truth, that they might be saved. And for this reason God will send them strong delusion, that they should believe the lie, that they all may be condemned who did not believe the truth but had pleasure in unrighteousness." (2 Thessalonians 2:9-12)

Satan will use counterfeit miracles, signs and wonders, and every sort of evil that deceives. You can be certain that he will do his best to be better prepared than you are on the battlefield. Therefore, make all your preparations now. Ask the Holy Spirit to give you the armor, train you to use it, and give you the strength you need to win on the battlefield. Ask the Lord to send the seven Spirits of God to fight with you and for you both now and forever.

KNOW THIS: THE ENEMY IS DECEPTIVE AND TRICKY:

The enemy is limited to the spirit realm and cannot himself carry these weapons of warfare. So, he uses the knives and swords of those who have character defects and are easily deceived. He preys on the emotions of anger, offense, bitterness, and hatred to enlist people to come against the elect of God. If possible, he will even deceive the elect into doing his dirty work.

"When they were at the large stone which is in Gibeon, Amasa came before them. Now Joab was dressed in battle armor; on it was a belt with a sword fastened in its sheath at his hips; and as he was going forward, it fell out. Then Joab said to Amasa, "Are you in health, my brother?" And Joab took Amasa by the beard with his right hand to kiss him. But Amasa did not notice the sword that was in Joab's hand. And he struck him with it in the stomach, and his entrails poured out on the ground; and he did not strike him again. Thus he died." (2 Samuel 20:8-10)

Joab was so consumed with anger and bitterness that he opened his hedge of protection and became vulnerable to the enemy. He was being led by his negative emotions and could only think of revenge. Satan took full advantage of this opening and attempted to use Joab's murderous actions to block David from uniting the kingdom. Under the enemy's deception, Joab resorted to deception to carry out his plot. He pretended to be coming to Amasa in friendship, but this was only to allow him to get close enough to murder Amasa without a fight.

We must remain alert and understand that the enemy wants to use you in the same way. He will take advantage of any opening he finds in you. If you are struggling with unforgiveness, bitterness, anger, or resentment, be aware that you are vulnerable. You must deal with these areas of spiritual weakness and find armor to cover all your existing wounds. What we are trying to do in this training is to learn the enemy's tactics and techniques, and let God cover these areas of vulnerability for our protection. Above all, you must avoid being led into deception. You must know his wiles. Not so that you will fear him, but in order to remain alert and ready.

God does not give you a spirit of fear. All of this training is to build you up, strengthen you, comfort you, and give you faith to overcome fear. God continues to remind His people: "Do not be afraid!" David understood this. He was not afraid, but he knew that Goliath had plenty to fear. Goliath had picked a fight with God and David was God's instrument of war. So, David called out to Goliath:

"Then David said to the Philistine, "You come to me with a sword, with a spear, and with a javelin. But I come to you in the name of the Lord of hosts, the God of the armies of Israel, whom you have defied. This day the Lord will deliver you into my hand, and I will strike you and take your head from you. And this day I will give the carcasses of the camp of the Philistines to the birds of the air and the wild beasts of the earth, that all the earth may know that there is a God in Israel." (1 Samuel 17:45-47)

One of President Thomas Jefferson's best known statements is: "The price of freedom is eternal vigilance." He learned this from experience, and it was a costly way to learn. We would be wise to learn the lesson from his experience rather than our own. Paul put it this way:

"You are all sons of light and sons of the day. We are not of the night nor of darkness. Therefore let us not sleep, as others do, but let us watch and be sober. For those who sleep, sleep at night, and those who get drunk are drunk at night. But let us who are of the day be sober, putting on the breastplate of faith and love, and as a helmet the hope of salvation. For God did not appoint us to wrath, but to obtain salvation through our Lord Jesus Christ, who died for us, that whether we wake or sleep, we should live together with Him." (1 Thessalonians 5:5-10)

To remain free, we can never let down our guard. Staying alert and ready takes energy. We need some spiritual drill sergeants to help us stay ready. Perhaps you are one of these special soldiers who can train, equip, and prepare the saints for the ministry of the church. Perhaps you are one who can help others in the body of Christ to stay focused, ready and alert.

TRAIN, PREPARE, GET IN SHAPE, AND BE READY FOR WAR!

I really like the quote below from Jeremiah. I like to read it aloud with as much energy and enthusiasm as possible. This is the battle cry we all need to hear as a motivation for the tasks ahead. I urge you to also read it aloud with emphasis.

"Order the buckler and shield, and draw near to battle! Harness the horses, and mount up, you horsemen! Stand forth with your helmets, polish the spears, put on the armor! Why have I seen them dismayed and turned

173

back? Their mighty ones are beaten down; They have speedily fled, And did not look back, For fear was all around," says the Lord." (Jeremiah 46:3-5)

It is not enough to merely get ready once. You have to stay ready at all times. Like we see in the story of Nehemiah, the church needs to have a division of labor. Half are at watch while half do the work.

"So it was, from that time on, that half of my servants worked at construction, while the other half held the spears, the shields, the bows, and wore armor; and the leaders were behind all the house of Judah." (Nehemiah 4:16)

And those who did the work used one hand to work while using the other to hold their weapons. Imagine trying to work with a sword girded on your waist.

"Those who built on the wall, and those who carried burdens, loaded themselves so that with one hand they worked at construction, and with the other held a weapon. Every one of the builders had his sword girded at his side as he built. And the one who sounded the trumpet was beside me." (Nehemiah 4:17-18)

That was not easy for the people in Nehemiah's day and it is not easy for us. They could do it, because they knew the threat was real. For Nehemiah, it cost half of the workforce. Yet, God blessed them and they were able to build the wall in record time.

The only way people are motivated to wear armor is to believe that the threat is real and imminent. This is difficult to say the least when they cannot perceive a real enemy and an imminent threat. However, you must realize that you do have a real enemy and there is a real threat. Every day the enemy is launching attacks against you as well as everyone and everything you love. The threat is real, but many people do not perceive it as real. One of your missions is to help people open their eyes to the truth in the spiritual realm and then to keep them open.

Healthy soldiers are combat multipliers. Just 100 years ago there were more combat casualties from disease and infections than bullets. Many wars have been lost because of sickness and disease. But remember that we are in a war we cannot afford to lose.

> *"And do this, knowing the time, that now it is high time to awake out of sleep; for now our salvation is nearer than when we first believed. The night is far spent, the day is at hand. Therefore let us cast off the works of darkness, and let us put on the armor of light. Let us walk properly, as in the day, not in revelry and drunkenness, not in lewdness and lust, not in strife and envy. But put on the Lord Jesus Christ, and make no provision for the flesh, to fulfill its lusts."* (Romans 13:11-14)

Heed Paul's advice to the Romans: it is time to wake up. It is critical to know the times and understand what to do. War has already been declared and there are many casualties all around us. It is time to report for duty in full battle armor.

ADDITIONAL SCRIPTURES FOR FURTHER STUDY

Luke 11:17-22, "But He, knowing their thoughts, said to them: "Every kingdom divided against itself is brought to desolation, and a house *divided* against a house falls. If Satan also is divided against himself, how will his kingdom stand? Because you say I cast out demons by Beelzebub. And if I cast out demons by Beelzebub, by whom do your sons cast *them* out? Therefore they will be your judges. But if I cast out demons with the finger of God, surely the kingdom of God has come upon you. When a strong man, fully armed, guards his own palace, his goods are in peace. But when a stronger than he comes upon him and overcomes him, he takes from him all his armor in which he trusted, and divides his spoils."

2 Corinthians 6:3-10, "We give no offense in anything, that our ministry may not be blamed. But in all *things* we commend ourselves as ministers of God: in much patience, in tribulations, in needs, in distresses, in stripes, in imprisonments, in tumults, in labors, in sleeplessness, in fastings; by purity, by knowledge, by longsuffering, by kindness, by the Holy Spirit, by sincere love, by the word of truth, by the power of God, by the armor of righteousness on the right hand and on the left, by honor and dishonor, by evil report and good report; as deceivers, and *yet* true; as unknown, and *yet* well known; as dying, and behold we live; as chastened, and *yet* not killed; as sorrowful, yet always rejoicing; as poor, yet making many rich; as having nothing, and *yet* possessing all things."

Proverbs 2:6-8, "For the LORD gives wisdom; from His mouth *come* knowledge and understanding; He stores up sound wisdom for the upright; *He is* a shield to those who walk uprightly; He guards the paths of justice, and preserves the way of His saints."

NOTES

LESSON 7

"KNOWING THE CHAIN OF COMMAND"

During one assignment, a South Korean General was visiting at our installation, and my wife, who was born and raised in Korea, was asked to help his wife with shopping and to translate for her as she met with the American Generals' wives. This all went very well and we really forgot about it until I was assigned to Korea again. I was contacted by the General's US Army liaison officer inviting us to have dinner with the General and his wife in their home. Over several days, all the protocol issues were resolved, and we met in their home for dinner.

After dinner, the General proudly showed us some of his prized possessions. He had acquired some beautiful and very expensive "mother-of-pearl" furniture which I enjoyed seeing. Moving from room to room, we admired his collections, and ended the tour with a visit to his home office. In the office, he had a very large collection of swagger sticks. These are decorative short staffs which are often carried by commanders as a symbol of authority. If you saw the movie, Patton, you may remember that he carried a swagger stick in the movie. The general had 40 or 50 of these sticks.

On the walls of his office, the general pointed to pictures of various presidents of South Korea presenting him with some of these swagger sticks as he assumed new command positions. These were a source of great pride for him and I very politely praised each one. Then he held one tightly in both hands in front of his chest and said. "You don't really understand the power and authority of a general in the Korean Army. You don't even have an English word for it." He paused for a moment and then went on, "Oh! Yes you do have a word for it: 'GOD!'" He swelled with pride to allow me time to take all of this in. Then it became clear that I was really beneath the level to be there and our time was over. He had been very polite and repaid the favor my wife had shown to his wife, and now it was time to politely excuse ourselves and leave.

I have reflected on that meeting many times, because there are some key lessons in the experience. All military units have established lines of authority and the power which goes with that authority is clearly defined. In the US Army, the authority and power are there, but the limitations are also made clear. No one is like God! No one truly possesses that level of power and authority over other people. In the US Military training and doctrine, there is an additional element somewhat unique. These Commanders are expected to be servant leaders, because their ultimate purpose is to serve and protect the nation and all those who are under their leadership.

MILITARY UNITS MUST HAVE CLEAR LINES OF AUTHORITY

In the military, these lines of authority are called the "chain of command." It is a military maxim that along with the authority and power comes an awesome responsibility. The higher you go in the chain of command the greater the level of responsibility. Promotion potential limits how high each can climb the ladder of success. People only move up to the highest level at which they are capable of carrying out their responsibilities. If they are promoted above their ability to work responsibly, problems begin to emerge which often lead to a termination of service.

Every chain of command is driven from the top down. At the top, general officers do decision briefings all the time. They are not brought in to work on problems, but to decide between alternative plans. Their staff principles work on problems and present the three best alternative plans. Then the general officer or highest level commander makes the decision. This decision, in effect, becomes law for that operation. These decisions are then sent down to subordinate levels for implementation. At the lower levels, the task is not to question or re-decide issues, but to take the actions necessary to accomplish the assigned missions.

One rainy morning, the Post Commander (a 2 star general) came in soaking wet. He was wet partially because soldiers in the US Army are not allowed to carry umbrellas while in uniform. As he came in the door, he was grumbling under his breath about the distance from the parking lot to the door (even though his spot was the closest to the door). He complained (to no one specifically) that the parking lot should be closer so people wouldn't get soaking wet walking in. At the end of the day, when he stepped through the door, he was shocked to see heavy equipment clearing the ground and making preparations for a new parking lot next to the building. He was very upset because he had worked all day on budget reductions and now had to pay the bill for a new parking lot. He stepped back inside and demanded to know who authorized this project. To his surprise everyone said, "You did sir!" He demanded to know when he had authorized this. It was quickly explained that as he came in that morning, he had demanded a parking lot closer to the door and made it sound so urgent that it was initiated immediately. Other projects had been stopped to address this urgent problem. An important lesson in leadership and the chain of command was learned by everyone that day. It was an expensive lesson, and this made it stick in all our minds, even to this day.

Every soldier is required to know the chain of command all the way to the top: the Commander in Chief, the President of the United States. Many organizations post the pictures of all the key people in the chain of command along with their names from the President down to the local commander. While I was in the Reserve Officers' Training Corps in college, we were required at all inspections to be able to name everyone in our chain of command. As far removed as I was from these people, I had to know the names of the Secretary of the Army, the Army Chief of Staff, and etc. down to my local commander.

One of the first and most difficult challenges in military training is to teach new recruits to recognize, respect, and follow the "chain of command." They must learn very quickly to recognize all of the rank insignia and know which to salute and how to give proper verbal greetings. At first this task seems overwhelming and the various rank insignias seem endless, but soon every soldier knows them. Brand new privates try to take the easy way out by saluting everyone who is not a private, because they all outrank him. But, soon he/she learns not to salute other enlisted soldiers even if they are high ranking. This training is normally presented in a very loud voice by a drill sergeant standing face to face with the terrified soldiers.

As a chaplain for a basic training unit, I was familiar with the struggle of many young men and women to adapt to this environment. They all had to struggle with this first big challenge of recognizing the various military ranks. In addition to written training materials, signs were placed along the sidewalks with the name and insignia for each rank. Soldiers had to quickly memorize them and show proper military courtesy to all officers.

Generals and some Colonels in command positions have automobiles which display their rank on the front bumper.

The rank is only posted on vehicles when that officer is actually inside. These vehicles must be saluted in the same way the officer would be saluted. One day a very frustrated soldier came to see me. He was extremely upset, because he had failed to salute the general's car. The car had stopped immediately and the general's aide spent several embarrassing minutes criticizing this young soldier in public. The young soldier, filled with sadness, embarrassment, and confusion, looked up at me, and said, "It was bad enough having to salute every officer, but now I have to salute cars! Where does it all end?"

There are many big challenges you must face as you move from organizations with a great deal of individual freedom of choice into an authority based system. This situation is exacerbated by the fact that many people today resent and reject authority. The "counter-culture" of the previous generation has become the standard culture of today. People are suspicious of authority and question orders, believing that they always have the option of saying no to their leaders. This cannot be tolerated in a military unit which by definition is a warrior based organization in which orders must be followed immediately. Those who join the military discover to their surprise that they have entered a different culture with different norms, rules, and penalties for violating the cultural taboos.

During any battle, "command and control" is a critically important element for successfully accomplishing the mission. Many military writers and historians use the phrase "the fog of war." This refers to the confusion and disorientation which can be experienced during combat operations. When bullets are flying and bombs are bursting, confusion takes over in the minds of almost everyone on the battlefield. In an environment experiencing this intensity of emotions filled with a drive to survive, clear lines of command are essential to success on the battlefield. People must be trained and made ready to respond immediately to all legal orders so that goals can be accomplished and the unit can maximize its potential for positive outcomes during rapidly sifting battlefield situations. If one soldier refuses to respond, others may die because of his/her disobedience. One of the greatest challenges leaders must face is the task of persuading people to value the welfare of the unit above their individual safety and survival. Eventually, they learn that failing to follow orders will also increase the likelihood that they may personally become a casualty of war.

It is critically important to have clear lines of authority, and to train people to follow these lines in spiritual warfare. The enemy will exploit every weakness in your organization. He seeks out people with a rebellious spirit, because he knows how much damage they can do to their units. The enemy constantly probes your forces to find weaknesses he can exploit by sending oppressive spirits to work against you and your objectives. He knows that soldiers who do not respond to commands jeopardize the mission and the lives of their fellow warriors. People who will not follow their leaders are of great potential benefit to the accomplishment of the enemy's plans. Therefore, it is critically important to teach and to learn these lessons and to know the lines of authority in your unit.

GOD ESTABLISHED CLEAR LINES OF AUTHORITY

As you carefully study the scriptures, you can clearly see that God has established at least seven (7) Levels of Authority in His command structure. Authority in the kingdom of God is driven from the top down as we have seen in military organizational structures. God has made the big decisions and has given His orders in the form of commandments, statutes, decrees and laws. Now, it is your job to obey the orders and accomplish the mission as directed. I have listed below these seven levels of authority from the highest to the lowest. They are:

(1). God (Father, Son, and Holy Spirit) (Psalm 47:9) (Matthew 28:18)

(2). Archangels (Rev 18:1) (Jude 1:8-11)

(3). Angels (2 Peter 2:11)

(4). Church with its 5-fold offices of ministry (Ephesians 4:11-16)

(5). Family (Ephesians 5:20-33)

(6). Government (Titus 3:1-3)

(7). Disciples over enemy authority (Luke 10:18-19, James 4:7)

All authority in heaven and earth ultimately rests with God. But for now, He has delegated much of that authority to others in His chain of command. Even though He retains ultimate control over all delegated authority, it is still the primary responsibility of Adam's descendents to manage the affairs of earth; always subordinate to God's authority. God delegated a great deal of authority to Adam in the Garden of Eden, but Adam didn't handle it well. He rebelled and fell from that high level of dominion and authority over the earth. And now, the Lord has delegated much of that authority to us. The psalmist proclaimed, *"The heaven, even the heavens, are the Lord's; but the earth He has given to the children of men."* (Psalm 115:16) Jesus took that authority (which Adam had surrender) back from Satan and returned it to us as evidenced in Matthew 28:

"And Jesus came and spoke to them, saying, 'All authority has been given to Me in heaven and on earth. Go therefore and make disciples of all the nations, baptizing them in the name of the Father and of the Son and of the Holy Spirit, teaching them to observe all things that I have commanded you; and lo, I am with you always, even to the end of the age.' Amen." (Matthew 28:18-20)

Great leaders know how to delegate authority. As the greatest leader, God is also the best delegator of power and authority.

As a great leader, Jesus delegated some of His authority down to us. Then we see Paul stating this even more clearly as he wrote to Titus, "Speak these things, exhort, and rebuke with all authority. Let no one despise you." (Titus 2:15, NKJV)

Father God delegated great authority to Jesus which belongs to Him until the end of time on this earth. "And Jesus came and spoke to them, saying, *"All authority has been given to Me in heaven and on earth."* (Matthew 28:18) However, when the end comes, Jesus will return it to Father God. *"Then comes the end, when He delivers the kingdom to God the Father, when He puts an end to all rule and all authority and power."* (1 Corinthians 15:24)

The end has not yet come. So, Jesus continues to exercise that authority during the church age. Even in this age, He knows the limitations of His authority. Jesus understands the source of His authority and remains respectful and obedient to the desires of the Father. We see this distinctly in Jesus words recorded in John 14.

> *"Do you not believe that I am in the Father, and the Father in Me? The words that I speak to you I do not speak on My own authority; but the Father who dwells in Me does the works."* (John 14:10)

Angels who are sent to represent God may also have great authority delegated to them for the accomplishment of their assigned mission. Responding to God's commands, they have His authority behind their words and actions. John saw an angel in heaven who had great authority which had been given to him to accomplish God's purposes. When God gives directives, He gives the authority to go along with them.

> *"After these things I saw another angel coming down from heaven, having great authority, and the earth was illuminated with his glory."* (Revelation 18:1)

Angels also know the limitations of their authority. There are some things they know they are not supposed to do, and we could learn a lot from their obedient responses. How many of us are as careful with our authority as they are with theirs. Many people in the church get involved in making accusations against other believers even though God's word forbids this. This is an area where angels avoid that mistake. Look closely at what Peter said about this. "*...whereas angels, who are greater in power and might, do not bring a reviling accusation against them (wicked people) before the Lord.*" (2 Peter 2:11) They know that this is the work of Satan. They are very clear about the fact that Satan is the accuser of the brethren. If you get involved in making accusations, you are actually doing Satan's work. You are in agreement with him, and that can result in great harm coming on other believers. We often step outside our area of authority, but angels stay within the limits of their authority.

> "*Yet Michael the archangel, in contending with the devil, when he disputed about the body of Moses, dared not bring against him a reviling accusation, but said,* "*The Lord rebuke you!*" (Jude 1:9)

To be battle ready, we must know and follow the lines of authority which God has established. We need to listen to His voice and follow all of His commands. Some people admit that they don't hear Him speaking or know His voice. But, Jesus clearly stated that His sheep would know His voice and follow Him. Many in the body of Christ need to break free from man-made rules and follow what Jesus said. This is an area where you need to ask the Holy Spirit to release the gift of discerning spirits to you. Then you must listen to Him; practice knowing His voice; and then make a commitment to follow His commands immediately and without question. We are at war, and good soldiers in wartime follow their leaders.

Another thing you can learn from the military is to train everything step by step. The training strategy of the military is to begin with the most simple skills and train them step by step with lots of repetition and practice. Then you move to a more difficult skill and follow the same process. Periodically you go back to the previously learned skills and practice them again in order to stay proficient. You need to do the same in your training for spiritual warfare. Begin by practicing the small things so they become easy and natural for you. Then when it is critically important, they are the natural response for you to give. Always remember: Immediate obedience is critical to winning the victory.

THERE ARE ALSO 7 LEVELS
OF ENEMY AUTHORITY

As we have seen before, the enemy counterfeits everything of God. If God establishes seven levels of authority, you can be certain that the enemy will do the same. This is most clearly seen in John's Revelation and in Paul's letter to the Ephesians. In these scriptures we get a clear picture of the lines of authority the enemy has adopted. Many are identified in Paul's letter to the church in Ephesus.

> *"For we do not wrestle against flesh and blood, but against principalities, against powers, against the rulers of the darkness of this age, against spiritual hosts of wickedness in the heavenly places."* (Ephesians 6:12)

These seven clearly defined levels of enemy authority are:
- (1). Satan
- (2). In the Last days: Beast (Rev 13:2, Rev. 17:12-14) and False Prophet
- (3). Principalities
- (4). Powers

(5). Rulers of the darkness of this age

(6). Spiritual hosts of wickedness in heavenly places.

(7). Serving demons who oppress

The enemy operates with false authority. He has borrowed or stolen authority from people who are weak and deceived. You must always remember that he is a liar and the father of lies. He lies about everything and this includes his authority. He is such a bold liar that he lied to Jesus face to face, and he lied to Jesus through others many additional times. Jesus saw through it and confronted him with the truth. However, Satan did not change because his course is already determined and there is nothing he can do about it. All he did in response to Jesus was to go away to wait for a more convenient time.

"And the devil said to Him, "All this authority I will give You, and their glory; for this has been delivered to me, and I give it to whomever I wish. Therefore, if You will worship before me, all will be Yours." (Luke 4:6-7)

Satan was claiming authority that was not his. You know that all authority in heaven and earth belongs to the Father. You know that it is the Father who decides who will receive it. At that time in His ministry, Jesus knew that this authority was already reserved for Him by Father God. It would all be His after He won the victory on the cross. I believe Satan was genuinely surprised by this. He had lied for such a long time that he started to believe his own false testimonies. In the past, this lie had worked on other people and he assumed it would work with Jesus. He was very mistaken in this belief.

This teaching about the false authority of the devil is very difficult for some people to accept, because they have been attributing power to Satan for such a long time. Some have argued and pointed to the following passage from Paul's writings.

"But even if our gospel is veiled, it is veiled to those who are perishing, whose minds the god of this age has blinded, who do not believe, lest the light of the gospel of the glory of Christ, who is the image of God, should shine on them." (2 Corinthians 4:3-4)

This is an isolated quote and so often taken out of context. Paul was speaking of the great deception which has covered the eyes of so many. The Word says that all forms of idolatry have demonic spirits behind their idols and false gods. The more often people worship false gods the more they make the demon behind them (Satan) a god in this world. But this is only part of the truth. A much greater truth is revealed in Psalm 82:6, *"I said, "You are gods, and all of you are children of the Most High."* Jesus used this quote (John 10:34-36 shown below) and said it was true when he confronted those who accused Him of blasphemy for claiming to be the Son of God. It is also true for you. You are supposed to be one of the gods (little g) of this world living and working in the authority God has given to you. You are supposed to have dominion over this world as you work in obedience to the Father. Don't give too much authority to the devil. Listen carefully to how Jesus explained this:

"Jesus answered them, Is it not written in your law, 'I said, You are gods'? If He called them gods, to whom the word of God came (and the Scripture cannot be broken), do you say of Him whom the Father sanctified and sent into the world, 'You are blaspheming,' because I said, 'I am the Son of God'? (John 10:34-36)

Considering these two references and Jesus' affirmation of its truth, you are as much of a god of this world as Satan. In addition, the authority you have been given is legitimate. It is authority you have received from God after it was won back through Christ. That should be the end of the matter, but many people continue to give their authority back to Satan. They do this by two primary means. First, any form of idolatry gives your authority back to Satan. Examine your life and see if you have put any part of the creation above the creator in your love and devotion. The second way people do this is through their confessions. How many times have you listened to people tell you all the ways the devil has blocked them, made them sick, hurt their family members, or caused great problems in the church. Instead of confessing the enemy's power, they should be making decrees to break his power and kick him out of their part of the garden. When they do this, they are attributing power to him as they give up their own authority. We must stop doing this.

The enemy counterfeits everything God does and everything the Lord possesses, and this includes authority. He wants you to believe in his false power and illegitimate authority. The testimony of many believers and intercessors seems to attribute more power to him than they do to God. We know that he can do false signs and wonders to help him win a following. We know that this will go to a whole new level when the Antichrist and False Prophet are manifested. Even this power is not theirs. They receive it in measure from God so that He can fulfill His plan and purpose.

Be on guard! The enemy deceives and twists words and concepts to gain back authority and power from you. Don't fall for it. He lies to make you believe what he is saying. Don't listen to his lies. Go back to the Word and start confessing God's truth. A couple of good places to go are Luke 10:19 and James 4:7. You must have these memorized and stored in your heart so they are always available as swords of the Spirit.

The enemy has extremely limited authority. He doesn't even have the keys to his own house or realm any more. Jesus took them away from him, and he is now keyless. Even during the great tribulation, he will only have the power God allows him to have. He has to come to God and ask permission to

A Warrior's Guide to THE SEVEN SPIRITS OF GOD

use power and authority against any believer. Remember how Jesus explained to Peter that Satan had asked to sift him like wheat. When Satan arrives with all his ugly lies and accusations, there is Jesus pleading your case. Who do you think the Father will listen too most?

> *"The ten horns which you saw are ten kings who have received no kingdom as yet, but they receive authority for one hour as kings with the beast. These are of one mind, and they will give their power and authority to the beast. These will make war with the Lamb, and the Lamb will overcome them, for He is Lord of lords and King of kings; and those who are with Him are called, chosen, and faithful."* (Revelation 17:12-14)

Notice from this passage that he gets his power and authority from the ten kings. They foolishly give it up, and perish when they try to get it back. Even with all his power and authority stolen from people, he is still limited. His authority is limited in size, scope, and significance. Don't believe his lies. Take back your authority. How much do you have? According to Jesus in Luke 10:19, you have authority over "ALL" his power. Live, work, and minister, in accordance with what Jesus said and not what the enemy says.

> *"Then I saw another beast coming up out of the earth, and he had two horns like a lamb and spoke like a dragon. And he exercises all the authority of the first beast in his presence, and causes the earth and those who dwell in it to worship the first beast, whose deadly wound was healed."* (Revelation 13:11-12)

The enemy's authority is limited in time. Remember the words of the demon possessed men who ran and fell down at Jesus' feet. The demons knew they only had a little while.

They frightened people, but Jesus frightened them, because they knew who He was, and they understood His authority. They knew that their authority was illegitimate, but His was authentic and powerful beyond anything in all of creation.

> *"When He had come to the other side, to the country of the Gergesenes, there met Him two demon-possessed men, coming out of the tombs, exceedingly fierce, so that no one could pass that way. And suddenly they cried out, saying, "What have we to do with You, Jesus, You Son of God? Have You come here to torment us before the time?"* (Matthew 8:28-29)

The devil only gets to do the really powerful things for a little while during the final period of the last days. Remember that this is why he is so angry and determined to destroy you. But look at what John says. "They overcame Him." He didn't stand a chance, because they had two very powerful weapons to us against him. He may be in a fury, but you can overcome him with "the blood of the Lamb" and with "the word" of your testimony.

> *"They overcame him by the blood of the Lamb and by the word of their testimony; they did not love their lives so much as to shrink from death. Therefore rejoice, you heavens and you who dwell in them! But woe to the earth and the sea, because the devil has gone down to you! He is filled with fury, because he knows that his time is short."* (Revelation 12:11-12)

The enemy's authority is limited in terms of space. At this time, he can only work in the "sons of disobedience." If you are in obedience to the Word of God and to the commands of Jesus, he has no ability to harm you. You have been raised to live with Jesus and even death has no more power over you.

Get into obedience and stay in obedience and the devil cannot work in you!

> *"And you He made alive, who were dead in trespasses and sins, in which you once walked according to the course of this world, according to* **the prince of the power** *of the air, the spirit who now works in the sons of disobedience."* (Ephesians 2:1-2)

Right now, the enemy is exercising authority which is actually yours. Have you ever loaned tools to a neighbor, friend or relative and then find that you can't get them back. They are using your tools to do their work. This is what Satan is doing in this age. But, here is some good news. Your big brother, Jesus, went to the enemy's house and took back all your tools. Now, hold on to them and do not let the enemy get his filthy hands on your authority again. You can start now by taking control of you own tongue. Confess what the Word of God says and do not confess what the enemy says. Confess the power and authority of God and the victory won by Jesus.

> *"Then the seventy returned with joy, saying, "Lord, even the demons are subject to us in Your name." And He said to them, "I saw Satan fall like lightning from heaven. Behold, I give you the authority to trample on serpents and scorpions, and over all the power of the enemy, and nothing shall by any means hurt you."* (Luke 10:17-19, NKJV)

How much authority do you have over the power of the enemy? "<u>ALL</u>"! So, how is it that people keep getting beaten up by Him? Well he has all these really nasty little demon spirits (all those fallen angels) working for him. The angel told John that these demons are foul spirits and unclean and hated birds. By their numbers and nastiness, they can be a nuisance, but they cannot be victorious unless you give your victory to them. Their kingdom has fallen, and they have been left without a home or place of safety. They're at your mercy.

> *"After these things I saw another angel coming down from heaven, having great authority, and the earth was illuminated with his glory. And he cried mightily with a loud voice, saying, 'Babylon the great is fallen, is fallen, and has become a dwelling place of demons, a prison for every foul spirit, and a cage for every unclean and hated bird!'"* (Revelation 18:1-2)

I want to decree that it is time to take back and hold on to what Jesus bought back for us with His blood! It is time to take the authority He has given us over all these foul spirits! It is time to wake up in the morning stepping on their necks and sending them into the pit. But, you can only do this if you understand your own authority. You can only do that if you accept it from Jesus and use it in accordance with the Word of God. Study the Word so that you can become an approved workman who rightly divides the time.

LEVELS OF HUMAN AUTHORITY

> *"For you can all prophesy one by one, that all may learn and all may be encouraged. And the spirits of the prophets are subject to the prophets. For God is not the author of confusion but of peace, as in all the churches of the saints."* (1 Corinthians 14:31-33)

I struggled with the above quote from Paul for a long time. I thought of many different meanings for this word which just didn't seem quite right. However, when I tied it to the idea of authority, it made sense. So many people relinquish their self control to others. They say things like, "He made me angry!"

That sounds plausible, but how is it that someone else has control over your emotions? I believe that you choose to be angry when someone behaves in a way you find offensive. If you claim control over your own emotions rather than giving it up to others you will begin to operating at a higher level of authority. In the same way that you control things in your soul, this verse says you have authority in the realm of the spirit. Our spirits are not out of control or in the hands of someone else. We are in charge of our own spirits, and we can choose how our spirit responds.

God delegated authority and dominion to Adam in the garden. After you came into the body of Christ, God delegated authority back to you in spirit, soul, and body. It is your task to have dominion over the spirit realm and to refuse to relinquish authority to the enemy. This is the base level of authority. How can you have authority over others if you can't control yourself and your emotions?

CHURCH AUTHORITY

God has further delegated very specific authority to church leaders for clearly defined reasons. The first order of business for the church is to equip the saints through teaching, training, mentoring, and supporting. They are to be equipped for the work of ministry and for building up the body of Christ. Paul clearly stated the levels of authority in the body of Christ (the church).

> *"And He Himself gave some to be apostles, some prophets, some evangelists, and some pastors and teachers, for the equipping of the saints for the work of ministry, for the edifying of the body of Christ,"* (Ephesians 4:11-12)

Ministerial authority or authority for ministry has been delegated to those leaders who are set apart by God in one or more of the 5-fold offices of ministry in the church. A great deal of power has been lost in the church because people are unwilling to accept this authority. When we refuse to accept God's chosen leaders, it is rebellion against the Lord first and then to these church leaders second. This is no different than Korah's rebellion.

"Likewise also these dreamers defile the flesh, reject authority, and speak evil of dignitaries. Yet Michael the archangel, in contending with the devil, when he disputed about the body of Moses, dared not bring against him a reviling accusation, but said, "The Lord rebuke you!" But these speak evil of whatever they do not know; and whatever they know naturally, like brute beasts, in these things they corrupt themselves. Woe to them! For they have gone in the way of Cain, have run greedily in the error of Balaam for profit, and perished in the rebellion of Korah. (Jude 1:8-11)

Jude gives a very clear statement about rebellion against God and its consequences. The spirit which was operating in Korah did not die when the ground swallowed the man alive. There was an oppressive demon present in that rebellion which still exists. This oppressive demon was still present as the writing of the New Testament came to a close. And, it is still present today because the New Testament churches were types of the churches in our present time.

The same problems manifesting in the churches recorded in Jude and Revelation are clearly present and active in the church today. People resist authority and easily get caught up in rebellion. The idea behind Korah's actions was that he was just as capable as Moses. Perhaps that was true, but Korah was not anointed by the Lord for the job. It is the "anointing" which we must respect and honor. We need to respect it as much as David did when he refused to speak out or strike out against Saul, even when Saul was trying to kill him.

People today seem to be in that same kind of rebellion against the anointing. They claim that this has somehow been made acceptable through Jesus, but this is very far from the truth. It is not consistent with Jesus teaching, and it is not consistent with the rest of the Word of God. The Word says twice, *"Touch not mine anointed, and do my prophets no harm."* (Psalm 105:15, and 1 Chronicles 16:22) Rebellion is just as offensive to God today as it was when Korah initiated it against Moses, and the consequences are the same. The consequences which are due to people today have been delayed during this period of grace. This is to allow people time to repent, but these consequences remain for those who do not repent and return to the authority established by God.

FAMILY AUTHORITY

God established lines of authority in families. Without lines of authority, organizations, large or small, fall into chaos. Perhaps this is why the family is under so much attack today. People in the body of Christ have refused to honor God's plan and God's established lines of authority. Closely study the full meaning of family lines of authority in the passage below.

> *"Wives, submit to your own husbands, as is fitting in the Lord. Husbands, love your wives and do not be bitter toward them. Children, obey your parents in all things, for this is well pleasing to the Lord. Fathers, do not provoke your children, lest they become discouraged."* (Colossians 3:18-21)

Many people today do not want to follow these lines of authority. Many men want to be liberated from them because they don't want to be responsible for their wives and children. Many women want to be liberated from over-bearing unloving husbands and from their responsibility for their children. Children want to be liberated from their parents because the spirit of rebellion persuades them to be in charge of their own lives. The problem in all these cases is the rejection of authority and the accompanying loss to the power of the anointing on the church and its leaders.

We miss many family blessings through this disobedience to God. People act as if God owes them blessings whether they are obedient or not. This is not a Biblical concept. We owe God our service, worship, and lives. We owe Him praise, blessings, honor, and majesty. We need to be grateful that He does not give us what we deserve. He gives us love, grace, and blessings in spite of who we are and what we have done. However, it is important to understand that the blessings and favor will not continue to flow into the lives of rebellious and disobedient people. Notice how Paul illuminates the meaning of one of the Ten Commandments. The way children honor their parents may determine the length of their lives and the blessings they will receive.

"Children, obey your parents in the Lord, for this is right. "Honor your father and mother," which is the first commandment with promise: "that it may be well with you and you may live long on the earth." (Ephesians 6:1-3)

AUTHORITY OF BELIEVERS

God gave all disciples, past and present, authority over the works of the devil.

"The seventy–two returned with joy and said, "Lord, even the demons submit to us in your name." He replied, "I saw Satan fall like lightning from heaven. I have

*given you **authority** to trample on snakes and scorpions
and to overcome all the power of the enemy; nothing
will harm you. However, do not rejoice that the spirits
submit to you, but rejoice that your names are written in
heaven."* (Luke 10:17-20, NIV)

This authority was not just for the 12 disciples as some have
claimed, but was for the larger group of disciples. In the NIV,
the number is translated as 72 rather than 70 disciples. I like the
prophetic meaning of these numbers. If you consider the original twelve plus six more sets of 12 (72), then you have 7X12
disciples. Seven is the number of completeness and twelve is
the number for governance. This speaks of the completeness of
authority over all the works of the devil. In John 14:12, Jesus
says, *"I tell you the truth, anyone who has faith in me will do
what I have been doing. He will do even greater things than
these, because I am going to the Father."*

The real meaning of the word translated as "anyone" in the
quote above is "anyone." It does not mean that only the first
twelve disciples had authority and power. We have already
seen that 84 (7X12) disciples had authority over the works of
the devil. Listen again to what Jesus said, "anyone who has
faith in me will do what I have been doing." If we have faith
in Jesus, you and I are included in this promise. Consider also
what Jesus said in His prayer to the Father after making this
promise:

*"I do not pray for these alone, but also for those who
will believe in Me through their word; that they all may
be one, as You, Father, are in Me, and I in You; that they
also may be one in Us, that the world may believe that
You sent Me. And the glory which You gave Me I have
given them, that they may be one just as We are one:"*
(John 17:20-22)

Have you believed in Jesus through the words of His disciples? Did you learn about Him through the words of Matthew, John, Peter, and etc.? If your answer is yes, then this promise has been given to you! You need to claim it and begin to operate in the power and authority which goes with it. Ask the Holy Spirit to guide you into the full understanding of this authority and send the seven Spirits of God to enforce the power.

GOVERNMENTAL AUTHORITY

"Let every soul be subject to the governing authorities. For there is no authority except from God, and the authorities that exist are appointed by God. Therefore whoever resists the authority resists the ordinance of God, and those who resist will bring judgment on themselves. For rulers are not a terror to good works, but to evil. Do you want to be unafraid of the authority? Do what is good, and you will have praise from the same." (Romans 13:1-3)

We are seeing rebellion against governments all over the World, today. Do you think that these rebellions have the Lord's blessing? Listen to what Jude says about people who respond this way. When the Bible was written, people were living under the control of brutal and cruel dictators. The same type of evil leaders today are not worse than those of olden days, and people are not living in worse conditions than the people in the Bible. Yet the word of God does not condone violent rebellion, and certainly not to establish an idolatrous brotherhood of power hungry despots.

"Likewise also these dreamers defile the flesh, reject authority, and speak evil of dignitaries." and *"Woe to them! For they have gone in the way of Cain, have run*

*greedily in the error of Balaam for profit, and perished
in the rebellion of Korah."* (Jude 1:8 & 11)

When we rebel against God's delegated authorities, we rebel against God. At times in the Bible cruel kings were established as part of God's justice to administer punishment to idolatrous people. Paul tells us to pray for them instead of rebelling against them. The Word clearly states that God can remove bad leaders at will and in His appointed times. Jude is saying that people actually perish because of their rebellion and disobedience.

I agree that life is much better when we have righteous leaders, but there is no assurance that rebellion will result in righteous leadership. In fact, history is replete with accounts of leaders rising up in the name of freedom who become more wicked and cruel than all the dictators from the past. Change for the sake of change is unwise and unproductive. It may even be disastrous.

*"When the righteous are in authority, the people rejoice;
But when a wicked man rules, the people groan."*
(Proverbs 29:2)

THE CHAIN OF COMMAND IS REAL
AND IT IS NECESSARY

Paul personally discovered the price of rebelling against God's authority which had been given to Jesus. He was blinded by a light from heaven and confronted by the very one he had persecuted.

*"And he said, "Who are You, Lord?" Then the Lord
said, "I am Jesus, whom you are persecuting. It is hard
for you to kick against the goads."* (Acts 9:5)

A goad is a sharp stick used to keep animals moving. Paul had foolishly been kicking against a sharp stick in the spiritual realm. It is very painful to kick something sharp because you have so many pain receptors in your feet. You cannot win a battle like that. It is similar to hitting your head against a brick wall. You don't do much damage to the stick or the wall, but you can do a lot of damage to your head and feet. Remember what Jesus is saying, When we rebel against God it is like kicking a sharp stick. You are not hurting God, but you may do some permanent damage to yourself.

We only have the authority which God has delegated for a little while. One day all authority will be handed back to Father God. At that time, we will all lay our crowns at the feet of Jesus and He will in turn give them all back to Father God.

"Then comes the end, when He delivers the kingdom to God the Father, when He puts an end to all rule and all authority and power." (1 Corinthians 15:24)

When this time comes, the day of judgment will also come. You need to ask yourself now, "Whose side have you been on? Are you on God's side or are you just on your own side? It is similar to what happens when you use a credit card, you have things to enjoy for now, but you are aware that a payment is coming due. Are you ready and able to pay the bill? I am going to need for Jesus to pay my bill. I am going to need the Father to accept that payment in place of mine. So, I have decided to side with Him now. How about you?

Right now, you have a chance to submit to His authority and be blessed. The Lord desires that everyone make the right choice and come to the knowledge of the truth. It is interesting and informative when you discover how much of this is tied to authority as it is in the passage below.

"Therefore I exhort first of all that supplications, prayers, intercessions, and giving of thanks be made for all men, for kings and all who are in authority, that we may lead a quiet and peaceable life in all godliness and reverence. For this is good and acceptable in the sight of God our Savior, who desires all men to be saved and to come to the knowledge of the truth." (1 Timothy 2:1-4)

Paul tells Timothy that submission results in godliness and reverence. Praying for leaders rather than rebelling against authority leads to quiet and peaceful lives. Peter sums it up this way, *"Honor all people. Love the brotherhood. Fear God. Honor the king."* (1 Peter 2:17)

Submission helps us to be good soldiers and win all of the spiritual battles day by day. Can you imagine an army made up of only rebellious people? There would be nothing but chaos, death, and destruction. Everyone would lose and no one would win. Good order and discipline are required for a functioning army and a winning team. On the battlefield, whether natural or spiritual, immediate obedience often means the difference between life and death. How you respond effects the lives of others around you. How you respond determines the level of trust God can place in you.

KEY CONCEPT: The chain of command is for the good of all concerned.

"Let all things be done decently and in order." (1 Corinthians 14:40)

ADDITIONAL SCRIPTURES FOR FURTHER STUDY

Mark 10:42-45, "But Jesus called them to *Himself* and said to them, "You know that those who are considered rulers over the Gentiles lord it over them, and their great ones exercise authority over them. Yet it shall not be so among you; but whoever desires to become great among you shall be your servant. And whoever of you desires to be first shall be slave of all. For even the Son of Man did not come to be served, but to serve, and to give His life a ransom for many.""

Numbers 27:18-20, "And the LORD said to Moses: "Take Joshua the son of Nun with you, a man in whom *is* the Spirit, and lay your hand on him; set him before Eleazar the priest and before all the congregation, and inaugurate him in their sight. And you shall give *some* of your authority to him, that all the congregation of the children of Israel may be obedient.""

Genesis 39:4, "So Joseph found favor in his sight, and served him. Then he made him overseer of his house, and all *that* he had he put under his authority."

John 12:49-50, "For I have not spoken on My own *authority;* but the Father who sent Me gave Me a command, what I should say and what I should speak. And I know that His command is everlasting life. Therefore, whatever I speak, just as the Father has told Me, so I speak."

James 4:7, "Therefore submit to God. Resist the devil and he will flee from you."

NOTES

LESSON 8

"WALKING IN RESURRECTION POWER"

I recommend that before you begin this lesson, read again one of the accounts of the resurrection of Jesus from the Bible. Read it aloud, because *"faith comes by hearing and hearing by the Word of God"* (Romans 10:17). One of the resurrection accounts is found in Luke 24.

"Now on the first day of the week, very early in the morning, they, and certain other women with them, came to the tomb bringing the spices which they had prepared. But they found the stone rolled away from the tomb. Then they went in and did not find the body of the Lord Jesus. And it happened, as they were greatly perplexed about this, that behold, two men stood by them in shining garments. Then, as they were afraid and bowed their faces to the earth, they said to them, "Why do you seek the living among the dead? He is not here, but is risen! Remember how He spoke to you when He was still in Galilee, saying, 'The Son of Man must be delivered into the hands of sinful men, and be crucified, and

the third day rise again.'" And they remembered His words." (Luke 24:1-8)

One of the things which really caught my attention as I read this passage in the NIV was the last sentence, *"Then they remembered his words."* I reflected on this and wondered how many times something similar had happened to others. When Peter heard the rooster crow the third time, then he remembered the words Jesus spoke. Why didn't he remember the first time or the second time? The disciples on the road to Emmaus didn't remember until after He broke the bread. Why is it so difficult for us to remember the words of Jesus? Why can't we remember them before we do something dumb like Peter did when he denied knowing Jesus three times?

There are some things which are simply too important for us to forget for even one moment. There are some words of Jesus that we must store in our hearts in order to be ready at all times to use them to fend off an enemy attack. There are some words from other parts of the Bible that we just can't risk forgetting even for a few seconds. We need to constantly read them aloud, and remind ourselves in order to keep them fresh in our memories. Begin now to make a list of power statements from the Word, and daily work on memorizing them. By doing this, you will get these important Biblical truths stored in your heart. You need to do this because you don't know the day or the hour of the next enemy attack.

I received this message from the Lord as I prepared for "Firstfruits Sunday." In the list of appointed times to meet with the Lord, one of those times was the "feast (appointed time) of firstfruits." This celebration was a rehearsal to help prepare people for the resurrection of Jesus Christ. The people had rehearsed this every year for thousands of years, but they didn't recognize it when it happened. Afterward, many remembered God's words.

I wonder how many people remember the Lord instructing Moses to have all Israel meet with Him at seven appointed times each year. The Lord told Moses that this was to be done for all generations. In other words, they were to do it for all time. From the beginning, Gentiles had a place in these meetings. Gentile nations are still expected to honor these appointments for all time by meeting the Lord in the same way as the Israelites. We hear this most clearly through the prophecy of Zechariah. The Lord instructed Zechariah to tell the people:

> *"And it shall come to pass that everyone who is left of all the nations which came against Jerusalem shall go up from year to year to worship the King, the LORD of hosts, and to keep the Feast of Tabernacles. And it shall be that whichever of the families of the earth do not come up to Jerusalem to worship the King, the LORD of hosts, on them there will be no rain."* (Zechariah 14:16-17)

These seven appointments were arranged so that people were only required to travel to the Temple three times each year. The three spring appointments were completed in eight days. This appointed time was at the barley harvest when people were to offer the firstfruits of their crops to the Lord. Fifty days later, they met again at the time of the wheat harvest for another firstfruit offering, called the feast of weeks or Pentecost. At this gathering, they rehearsed receiving the promise of the Father. It is important to note that Jesus sent the disciples to Jerusalem to wait for the "promise of the Father." Through the prophet Joel, God had promised to pour out His spirit on all flesh and it began to happen on that day, and it is still happening as new generations emerge. Remember the Spirit was to be poured out on all flesh. And finally, the three fall appointments also occur over a short period of time and can be celebrated in one visit. This meeting occurs at the end of the harvest of grapes and olives which later came to symbolize the promise of new wine and fresh oil in the kingdom of God for all people. These last three are rehearsals for the second coming of Christ.

In spite of centuries of rehearsals, the religious leaders and teachers were unable to recognize the fulfillment of the promise of firstfruits and missed the most important day in the history of planet earth. On this day, Jesus was raised from the dead as the firstfruits of all those who would inherit eternal life. This happened precisely on the day of Firstfruits. God's timing is always perfect.

When Jesus was raised from the dead, even the disciples didn't remember His words. He had told them about his death and resurrection over and over. And, like these disciples, we too can miss out on the movements of the Lord. We must remember and prepare. The purpose of the feast is to help us remember. Our failure to remember leaves us open to so many enemy attacks. It is good when you finally get it, and this happens by remembering His words. But, wouldn't it be better to remember before we fall? So, prepare now and be ready when it happens! Amen?

JESUS AS THE FIRSTFRUITS

"But now Christ is risen from the dead, and has become the firstfruits of those who have fallen asleep. For since by man came death, by Man also came the resurrection of the dead. For as in Adam all die, even so in Christ all shall be made alive. But each one in his own order: Christ the firstfruits, afterward those who are Christ's at His coming." (1 Corinthians 15:20-23)

I prefer to think of the day on which we celebrate Jesus' resurrection as "Firstfruits Sunday." It is no longer a rehearsal for something to come, but it is a remembrance of what God has already done for us. Jesus changed the Passover meal from a rehearsal to a remembrance when He told them to remember Him when they broke the bread and drank from the "Cup of Redemption."

The name Easter derives from an old English word Eastre which referred to a month long celebration of Eastre, the pagan goddess of Spring. This celebration was filled with fertility rites and was believed to curry the favor of the goddess for abundant crops and the healthy births of children and farm animals. The bunnies, chicks and eggs are all symbols of fertility, and fit in nicely with the celebration. This pagan festival was celebrated near the time the early Christians celebrated the resurrection. Over time the two merged and eventually the goddess was dropped and the focus was only on Jesus' resurrection. Every year, pastors face the challenge of explaining all this to people who want to know the origin of the name. I personally prefer to have the opportunity to explain the meaning of firstfruits and keep the focus on Jesus. It is so much easier to explain and validate it as "Firstfruits Sunday," because the resurrection actually occurred on the Day of Firstfruits.

The resurrection of Jesus is one of best documented events in human history. In spite of what you may hear from some cowardly and uninformed reporters on your favorite politically correct television programs, this is not just some unfounded belief by a group of people who have chosen to call themselves Christians. It is not a baseless man made belief like that espoused and supported by these same TV commentators. Any other fact in history, this well established would be confidently proclaimed as truth by the scientific community and the media. However the veil of deception is so tightly wrapped around the heads of pseudo intellectuals today that they frequently call truth a lie and a lie the truth.

The fact is that there were over 500 known witnesses to the resurrection of Jesus Christ. Over a period of 40 days, Jesus appeared to individuals, small groups, and to over 500 people on one occasion. Many of these people were still alive at the time the accounts in the New Testament were written. Yet, no one of that period of time contradicted this well known fact. It was so well known and documented in that time that the Sanhedrin which had condemned Jesus to death did not argue the point with His disciples when they were on trial at a later time.

Many priests and Pharisees could no longer deny who Jesus was because they knew He had been raised from the dead. It is recorded in Acts 6:7, *"Then the word of God spread, and the number of the disciples multiplied greatly in Jerusalem, and a great many of the priests were obedient to the faith."* When Paul met with the leaders of the church in Jerusalem to discuss circumcision for gentile believers, there was an entire party of Pharisees (who were believers) present at the meeting (Acts 15:5). In spite of this overwhelming evidence, many chose not to believe. They refused to believe as do many people today. The people then and people today are not persuaded by facts or clear evidence. There are more early manuscripts of the New Testament still in existence than any other writings in history. In spite of the fact that they are from different places and times, there are virtually no differences in these accounts. In the face of this overwhelming evidence, any person claiming to be Christian who speaks doubt from places of public trust should be covered with shame.

During this final lesson in advanced training, we will examine the advanced skill of using resurrection power. I want to apologize up front for calling this an advanced skill, because I will show you later that it is supposed to be a basic skill. However, we have distanced ourselves so much from this concept that it appears to be truly advanced. Somehow, over the centuries we have become retarded in some of the basic spiritual workings. We should be advanced, but we have to constantly go back to the basics due to a lack of faith and understanding. And, because of our current status in faith (or more precisely, the absence of faith), I must address it as an advanced skill.

When a sports team performs very badly in a game, what does the coaching staff normally do? Will they develop some elaborate new play requiring advanced skills and understanding and work all week to teach it? No! They go back to the basics. In their practice sessions, they will go back over all the basic skills of the sport and rehearse them until they become natural. At the next game, the fans are excited to see the change in their team and believe that they are now more highly advanced. In reality, the team has merely gone back to the basics of the sport. When you are out of sync, you need to go back to the basics. So here at the end of the training, we are going back to one of the most foundational teachings of the Bible. We need to constantly go back to and practice these basic things which will appear to many on game day to be advanced.

The idea of resurrection was not new to scripture or unusual compared to older writings in the Bible. We can go all the way back to the time of Abraham and discover that he believed in the resurrection.

> *"By faith Abraham, when he was tested, offered up Isaac, and he who had received the promises offered up his only begotten son, of whom it was said, "In Isaac your seed shall be called," concluding that God was able to raise him up, even from the dead, from which he also received him in a figurative sense."* (Hebrews 11:17-19)

Abraham had faith in God and he knew that when God said something it was going to happen. Now Abraham was faced with two seemingly contradictory statements from God. On the one hand, God promised that many nations would come through Isaac. Now, God said to sacrifice him. The only possible explanation in Abraham's mind was that God would raise

Isaac from the dead after he had sacrificed him. No wonder his faith was later accounted to him as righteousness.

It may be instructive to go over a list of the resurrections documented in the Bible. It builds faith to go over and over a list like the one below. Consider all these examples and let the Spirit build up your most holy faith which is a gift from the Lord.

> Elijah: raised the son of the Widow at Zarephath (1 Kings 17)
> Elisha: raised the son of the Shunammite woman (2 Kings 4)
> The man raised when his body touched Elisha's bones. (2 Kings 13)
> Ezekiel raised a valley of dry bones (Ezekiel 37)
> Jesus: raised the son of the widow from Nain (Luke 7)
> Jesus: raised Lazarus (John 11)
> Jesus: raised the daughter of Synagogue ruler, Jairus (Mark 5)
> Jesus Himself was raised from the dead (New Testament)
> Paul: raised a boy who fell from a 3rd floor window (Acts 20)
> Peter: raised Tabitha (Dorcas) (Acts 9)
> Many holy people were raised when Jesus died (Matthew 27)

I like to look at some of the Bible stories with fresh eyes. Sometimes we have heard them over and over and we just let things pass without notice. But, this story of those raised when Jesus died is very unusual and somewhat funny. When you read the story, notice that they came out of their graves at the moment Jesus died, but they did not go into town until Jesus was raised from the dead. I read that, and I started thinking about what happened in the mean time.

Can you imagine that scene today? Many graves suddenly open up at a local cemetery and many holy people come to life and just hang out around the cemetery for three days. Surely someone noticed them hanging around and told others. Can you imagine people in long lines going out to see this. Today, all the news channels would be out there with reporters asking every foolish question they could imagine. They would come up with some totally false concept, share it, and blame someone else for the error when they were proven wrong. It would be a media circus and clowns would be out in great numbers.

Then I wondered what were they doing for three days. Did they gradually get back all their muscles, tendons, and skin? Did they have to work out or go through physical therapy? Did they eat? And if so, what did they eat to get their strength back? Were they mending their old half rotten cloths? Or, were they being outfitted with new ones. This entire story is so unusual and doesn't seem to match with any of our normal concepts of reality. I can't help but think about and be amused by this Biblical scene in which dead people are raised to life and left hanging out in the cemetery for three days.

Then I wondered what it was like when they went into town. Can you imagine the response of the people who saw them and perhaps knew them when they were living. Someone might say, "Look there's old Moshe. I went to his funeral. What's he doing walking around 10 years later?" Now, imagine the impact of their testimony. Would you be impressed by talking with someone you knew had died many years ago, but was now alive and telling you about Jesus? Would it affect your belief system to see many people like that walking around and telling others about God, heaven, Jesus, and the resurrection?

And, what happened to them after that day? Did they die again? Did it happen right away? Did they go back to their graves, crawl in and let the dirt fall back over them? Or, did they live for several years giving testimony to Jesus' resurrection? I believe they lived, witnessed, and brought many to the Lord. No wonder the Sanhedrin kept quiet when Peter told them about the resurrection of Jesus. Many of them had probably seen some of these resurrected saints. Do you think they told these resurrected saints to stop talking about Jesus? I think not!

The problem with grasping resurrection power does not come from a lack of references in the scriptures. So, what is the problem? If the problem is not with the Bible, what is the problem? The problem is definitely with us and our lack of understanding and our loss of faith. It is much easier to teach a child to believe in the resurrection than to convince an adult. It is much easier to convince someone in a third world country that Jesus was raised than to persuade a theologian, because they are not filled with a spirit of religion which affirms a form of godliness but denies the power of the gospel.

Jesus had something to say about this. How many of you know that Jesus was not always seeker sensitive or politically correct? However, I would rather listen to Jesus than to all the sensitive, inclusive, and politically correct people on earth. How about you? Listen to what He said, and remember that He was saying this to the religious leaders and the so called experts in the law.

"Jesus answered and said to them, "You are mistaken, not knowing the Scriptures nor the power of God. For in the resurrection they neither marry nor are given in marriage, but are like angels of God in heaven. But concerning the resurrection of the dead, have you not read what was spoken to you by God, saying, 'I am the God of Abraham, the God of Isaac, and the God of Jacob'? God is not the God of the dead, but of the living." And when the multitudes heard this, they were astonished at His teaching." (Matthew 22:29-33)

People are still astonished by Jesus' teaching and unfortunately many just don't really believe it. They also struggle with the idea that God is the God of Abraham, Isaac, and Jacob, and they are still alive today. God does not have a memory wall in his house to display pictures of dead heroes from the Old Testament. God is not collecting dead disciples as trophies to keep in a case somewhere in heaven. He is currently resurrecting dead spirits as in the days of Ezekiel. We know that Moses is alive because he showed up on the Mount of Transfiguration some 1500 years after his death. We know that Elijah is alive because he was there as well.

Jesus constantly spoke about the resurrection of the dead. He left no doubt about the fact that God is raising His saints to everlasting life. Yet, people are still surprised, and many people who call themselves Christians do not believe in the resurrection. I have experienced people attacking me in church on Resurrection Sunday for preaching that this actually happened. We see the same unbelief in the disciples who were totally unsuspecting of Jesus' resurrection. They were all taken by surprise and struggled to believe it. It probably helped them to consult with some of those dead saints walking around town.

JESUS: MORE THAN A RECIPIENT
HE IS THE RESURRECTION!

"Jesus said to her, "I am the resurrection and the life. He who believes in me will live, even though he dies; and whoever lives and believes in me will never die. Do you believe this?" (John 11:25-26)

Jesus is so much more than just someone who happened to be raised from the dead. Jesus told Martha straight out that He is the resurrection and the life. When Jesus said "I am" that was the same as when God said it to Moses. Think about how powerful those two words are when spoken by Jesus. Do you remember when they came to arrest Jesus and He asked who they were looking for? *"They answered Him, "Jesus of Nazareth." Jesus said to them, "I am He." And Judas, who betrayed Him, also stood with them. Now when He said to them, "I am He," they drew back and fell to the ground."* (John 18:5-6) These rough tough soldiers and temple guards drew back and fell to the ground when Jesus said, "*I am!*" I have tried to imagine that scene and the tone of His voice when it carried that much power. This was not just a few soldiers. It was a detachment. And, they fell to the ground when He spoke two words. Think about it!

This statement, "*I Am,*" is about the eternal presence of the one who said it. He was in existence before the world was created! He is alive right now! And, He will be alive for all eternity! More than that, God has given Him the power of resurrection and life. It is in Him and it is Him! He is and always will be the resurrection and the life.

Those who believe in Him will live even if they die. Wow! That is good news! We have something wonderful to share with the world. So, why are we hanging back and not giving our testimony? Jesus went further with Martha and said, "*Whoever lives and believes will never die." Then, what did He say? He asked that very important question which so many want to avoid. He asked, "Do you believe this?*" What will you say when Jesus asks you that question?

We don't die when this temporary house we live in stops working. We just transition to a much greater experience of the life God has placed in us. We become the speaking spirits we were created to be with more power than we ever experienced while captured in this body. But the real question is: "Do you believe this?" We need to ask ourselves this question. Do we really believe it? Do we act like we believe it? Some people answer yes to the first question but no to the second question. We need to get our talk and our walk lined up.

Remember earlier when we reflected on what happened when Jesus died and graves opened allowing dead saints (holy people) to come back to life. Let's look at that again! I want you to consider another interesting point.

"*And Jesus cried out again with a loud voice, and yielded up His spirit. Then, behold, the veil of the temple was torn in two from top to bottom; and the earth quaked, and the rocks were split, and the graves were opened; and many bodies of the saints who had fallen asleep were raised; and coming out of the graves after His resurrection, they went into the holy city and appeared to many."* (Matthew 27:50-53)

All of these things happened after Jesus cried out in a loud voice. Now, normally someone that close to death from loss of blood and suffocation is not able to cry out with a loud voice. If He was strong enough to do this, He should have had the strength to live much longer. This speaks of Jesus being in total control of this event. He was not some helpless victim of big government gone wrong. This passage says "He gave up His spirit!" It was His to give up and it was His to take back! He was in charge. Now, I wonder what he said when he cried out in a loud voice. Many people make some big assumptions from other gospels and declare them to be true. But I have to wonder if that is what really happened. The church has taught that He only made seven statements on the cross. But, how do we know this?

When Jesus cried out in this loud voice, He started an amazing chain reaction that shook the entire region. Think about it! The earth shook, rocks split, the curtain of the temple was torn in two from top to bottom, tombs broke open, and holy people were raised from the dead! Whatever He said, it was powerful and it was effective. I remember hearing a preacher ask why Jesus said, "Lazarus, come forth!" instead of just saying, "Come forth!"? His answer was, "Because if He had only said, "Come forth!" every dead person on earth would have risen.

Power! We are talking about resurrection power. What kind of power does it take to raise a body dead for 4 days or for 3 days? Several people have asked me about the people who died in the twin towers on September 11, 2001. Many of them were vaporized. People want to know if God can raise them from the dead. My answer is absolutely "YES!" If he could raise those Holy people who had been dead for a very long time, he can raise the people who died on 9/11! If he can put flesh, skin, and life into those old bones which may have been dead for hundreds of years, He can raise you from the dead! Amen?

I want you to know that whatever that power is which raised all those people from the dead, God has given it to us. Do you believe that? Look at what Paul wrote to the Ephesian church:

"I pray also that the eyes of your heart may be enlightened in order that you may know the hope to which he has called you, the riches of his glorious inheritance in the saints, and his incomparably great power for us who believe. That power is like the working of his mighty strength, which he exerted in Christ when he raised him from the dead and seated him at his right hand in the heavenly realms," (Ephesians 1:18-20, NIV)

Paul says that this kind of resurrection power is for us who believe. Think about this! Paul is asking for our spiritual eyes to be opened so that we can be enlightened. Most people need a creative miracle in their spiritual eyes to get what Paul is saying. If we can get our eyes open, we will see three awesome things. First, we will know the "hope to which He has called" us. Most people don't have a clue about this hope to which they have been called. Second, we can know the riches of his glorious inheritance in the saints. Many Christians think you have to die to get your inheritance. This doesn't make any sense at all. You don't die to get an inheritance. You get it when someone else dies. You got it when Jesus died. Third, so we can know "his incomparably great power for us who believe." What kind of power is that? It is resurrection power! It is "like the working of his mighty strength, which he exerted in Christ when he raised him (Jesus) from the dead." Wow! But, then we have to face that same old question, "Do you believe this?"

If you really believe this, it should change some things in your world. But the problem is we say we believe it, but we don't really have that faith deep down inside. If you are struggling with this idea, watch out because there is still more. If the idea we have been discussing is difficult to accept, the next one may be an even greater challenge for you to grasp and accept.

GOD HAS GIVEN RESURRECTION POWER TO QUICKEN YOU

I am not referring to something that may or may not happen sometime in the distant future. The Lord has already done it! The resurrection brings back to life every dead hope, every dead dream, every lost possibility, and every dead thing in you. I love the stories of Smith Wigglesworth. A man who traveled with him told the story about trying to pin a flower on him, but found out that he didn't have a button hole on his suit jacket. And Smith would not let him pin the flower on him. He said, "As soon as that flower was cut it started to die, and I will not have anything that smells of death on me." I want to stand in faith with Mr. Wigglesworth on this point. I don't want anything that smells of death on me either, because I want to live in resurrection power. I want to experience the power of God in me that brings everything back to life.

> *"Blessed be the God and Father of our Lord Jesus Christ, who according to His abundant mercy has begotten us again to a living hope through the resurrection of Jesus Christ from the dead, to an inheritance incorruptible and undefiled and that does not fade away, reserved in heaven for you, who are kept by the power of God through faith for salvation ready to be revealed in the last time." (1 Peter 1:3-5*

Not only is the resurrection the power that gives us new birth, but it also resurrects the hope in our lives so that we can have "a living hope." Thanks be to the God and Father of our Lord Jesus Christ! Amen! You see, without His resurrection, none of these promises are for us. Paul explained it to the church in Corinth.

> *"If in this life only we have hope in Christ, we are of all men the most pitiable. But now Christ is risen from the dead, and has become the firstfruits of those who have fallen asleep."* (1 Corinthians 15:19-20)

The wonderful work God has done for us goes beyond all the things we have already considered. The resurrection is the doorway to your reward. Did you know that?

> *"But when you give a banquet, invite the poor, the crippled, the lame, the blind, and you will be blessed. Although they cannot repay you, you will be repaid at the resurrection of the righteous."* (Luke 14:13-14)

Jesus promises that full restitution of everything you have given will be made at the resurrection of the righteous. The doorway for this repayment is the resurrection. You will be repaid for what you have given for others. Everything you have ever shared will come back to you. So, we can confidently give now knowing that we will receive it back at that time. Nothing you do will ever be forgotten. Nothing will ever be overlooked, and you will receive everything back from the Lord. Thanks be to God! Amen?

And there is even more! Hallelujah! The resurrection is the powerful key to understanding how it is that we can become like Him. It's the resurrection which brings the understanding and the power.

"I want to know Christ and the power of his resurrection and the fellowship of sharing in his sufferings, becoming like him in his death," (Philippians 3:10, NIV)

In death we become like Him! Now by itself that wouldn't be very good news. We would just be dead. But the good news is that it is His death and not ours which makes all this possible. You don't have to die to become like Him. You become like Him in His resurrection through His death. Now, that's good news! We don't have to strive for it, because God does everything for us.

But, it doesn't stop here. The message of scripture goes even one step further. If we're like Him in death, we are also like Him in resurrection. Death is not the end for us. Death no longer has any hold on us. If we have already died with Christ, how can death be a threat any longer? However this takes us back to that challenging question Jesus asks. "Do you believe this?" It always comes back to this question doesn't it.

If you don't believe it, you can't live in the power of the resurrection or become like Him in his death. Without faith, it has no meaning. *"Now faith is the substance of things hoped for, the evidence of things not seen."* (Hebrews 11:1) And remember Hebrews 11:6 (NIV), *"And without faith it is impossible to please God, because anyone who comes to him must believe that he exists and that he rewards those who earnestly seek him."* Without faith, you simply cannot have the things God has reserved for you. Listen again to Jesus' question, "Do you believe this?"

As we read and study God's Word we see that all these promises just get better and better. Now, for some really GOOD NEWS: your resurrection has already occurred. You don't have to wait until you die to get it. You already have it by participating in it through Jesus.

"But God, who is rich in mercy, because of His great love with which He loved us, even when we were dead in trespasses, made us alive together with Christ (by grace you have been saved), and raised us up together, and made us sit together in the heavenly places in Christ Jesus, that in the ages to come He might show the exceeding riches of His grace in His kindness toward us in Christ Jesus." (Ephesians 2:4-7)

Paul declares that we have already been raised with Christ. The verb "raised" is in the past tense. It has already happened. Well, there is even better news. And again you will notice that the message is in the past tense which means it has already happened. The Lord has already "seated us with him in the heavenly realms." Right now, you have a seat in heaven. This sounds good, but we have to deal with that question again. Jesus asks, "Do you believe this?" Again this is the problem. There is no problem with the Bible. It is all true and has been validated by the resurrection of Jesus Christ. The problem is and always has been with us. Do we have sufficient faith to believe that the resurrection of Jesus Christ is also our resurrection? Do we believe the Word of God, and know with certainty that we are seated with Him in heavenly realms? Do you believe this?

If you believe this, then you must have a seat up there with Jesus. Right? And, if you have already been seated with Him, you must be able to go there and sit with Him from time to time. Right? Well there it is again. "Do you believe this?" Considering our struggles in believing, it sometimes seems odd that we are called "the believers." Some people believe, but they just believe so very little. They believe little and they also believe that so little of this is really theirs. What about you? Do you believe what the Word says or do you hold to what someone else taught you? Do you stand on the Word of God or on man-made doctrines? We were warned in the New

Testament that false teachers would come into our midst and lead us away from the power of God.

Well, I've decided to push this to the limit. I believe that you need to face up to the whole message. So, consider this:

GOD HAS GIVEN RESURRECTION POWER TO US FOR MINISTRY

Now, this is where many people will drop out. They can believe that Jesus raised the dead and that some of the apostles raised the dead. However, they draw the line at believing they can do the same. If you are like that, it is very difficult to believe what Jesus said. Because he said:

> *"Heal the sick, cleanse the lepers, raise the dead, cast out demons. Freely you have received, freely give."* (Matthew 10:8)

Since the time of the early church, people have struggled with accepting this level of anointing. But consider this: Jesus did not say pray for the sick. He said heal the sick. Jesus didn't say pray for the dead. He said raise the dead. Jesus did not say pray for lepers to be healed. He said cleanse them. He didn't say to explain away demon possession and pray for the mental health of people. He said to cast out demons. And, catch this: "Freely you have received..." Received what? You have received healing, cleansing, freedom from oppression, and you have been raised from the dead by participating in Jesus resurrection. You have also received the power of the resurrection to begin to be obedient to Christ's commands. So, go out there and raise some people from the dead. But, then that sticky question comes back. Jesus asks, "Do you believe this?" And, many say, "Well, Yes and No!" Do you remember what Jesus said in Matthew 5:37? *"But let your 'Yes' be 'Yes,' and your 'No,' 'No.' For whatever is more than these is from the evil one."*

Perhaps the problem is related to what we have received. Perhaps we have not been open to receiving these power gifts from the Lord. Perhaps you are remembering how He told the disciples to wait until they received power from on high. Perhaps that's what you are doing: just waiting for some power. This is a great safety net. If you haven't received it, you can't be expected to give it. Remember this: they didn't receive power because they waited. They waited for the appointed time of the Lord. That time has come and the prophecies have been fulfilled in all who truly believe. But, do you believe what Jesus said? You see, it is far past time to have received all these basic things from the Lord. When the Holy Spirit was released on the Day of Pentecost, He began to release anointing and gifting to all the disciples. He has not stopped doing that. He is doing it still and it is time for us to be open to receive it. Remember, it is to be poured out on all flesh, and that includes you.

Some people question the validity of such a claim. It goes against the things they have been taught. Some theologians make the claim that this was added later. If you ask who added it and when, they can't tell you. But, they don't like it so it must have been added by someone. This is the type of logic that breaks the power of our faith. When these people are confronted with these words from Jesus, they want to find a way out of believing and obeying. It goes against the claims of a powerless church which attempts to excuse why nothing is happening in their meetings, programs, and services.

But, listen to what Paul said to King Agrippa: *"Why should it be thought a thing incredible with you, that God should raise the dead?"* (Acts 26:8, KJV) According to Paul, resurrections should be the norm and not the incredible. Think about what the word incredible means. It means without credibility. And we are guilty of putting this question of credibility into so many of our statements about God. People speak of His incredible power. Do we intend to say that it is not credible? God's power is real, it is awesome, it is amazing, and it is credible.

So, it should not be thought strange or incredible that people are being raised from the dead. It should be the norm. But, here comes Jesus' question again, "Do you believe this?" What do you think He meant when He said, "raise the dead!" If you find yourself struggling to twist this around and to come up with something which sounds reasonable to the world, you probably don't really believe what Jesus said.

Think about it! If the word goes out today that someone has been raised from the dead what happens? People will mock the idea. Geraldo will show up. Right? He will show up with his crew and they will twist and turn everything to the point that when he airs the show, you look like a complete idiot. Isn't that what happens. You can see that it all becomes really incredible once the media shows up to spin it into a scandal.

There is great power connected with believing God this way. There is great power, because God's power is connected with it. Power is connected with the truth, and when you speak God's truth you release great power.

"And with great power the apostles gave witness to the resurrection of the Lord Jesus. And great grace was upon them all." (Acts 4:33)

The context here is the disciples gathering to pray for boldness in sharing the gospel. They had been released from jail and warned not to talk about the resurrection of Jesus. So, they had gathered to ask the Lord for boldness so they could overcome their fear of man and trust in Him alone. Look closely at the outcome of this kind of prayer. They received a second outpouring of the Holy Spirit. The house shook, and they were all given more power. Now, look at this and see what happens when you testify to the resurrection with great power. What is the result of this kind of witnessing? Much grace was upon all of them. Well, "Do you believe this?" Everything about the resurrection of Jesus brings us back to that question. You either believe it or you don't. If you don't, then you should expect a powerless life for Christ.

In the old TV show, Mission Impossible, each episode began by the team leader being told "Your mission, should you decide to take it, is…" In the same way we can say, "You mission, should you decide to take it, is to raise the dead!" I sometimes wonder if God is going to have to call forth another generation to use His power gifts effectively? Or, will He find some faithful disciples among us who are willing to obey all He has commanded? Over and over I have listened to people say they believe the Bible and that they believe what Jesus said. But, when you ask them about raising the dead, they begin to make excuses, give qualifiers, stammer and stutter before admitting that they don't believe it for their own lives and ministry. If you can honestly say you believe it, and you're really ready to do this, then:

IT'S TIME TO RAISE THE BAR AND
ESTABLISH A NEW NORM

Remember at the beginning of this lesson, I told you that I would later demonstrate that resurrection power is not actually an advanced skill. It is supposed to be a foundational doctrine and practice. But we have lost it through disuse and disbelief. Well, consider carefully what the writer of Hebrews is saying in the passage below.

"Therefore, leaving the discussion of the elementary principles of Christ, let us go on to perfection, not laying again the foundation of repentance from dead works and of faith toward God, of the doctrine of baptisms, of laying on of hands, of resurrection of the dead, and of eternal judgment." (Hebrews 6:1-2)

Think about it! The writer of Hebrews is saying that raising the dead is elementary. It is part of the foundational principles of what we are doing. It was not supposed to be an advanced skill. It should be the norm. It should be happening every day. But, because we have believed the false teachers, we've lost it, and now we can only think of it as an advanced skill.

We can make all kinds of excuses about the commands of Jesus. We can claim that it is for people more advanced than we are. We can state that it was only for the 12 apostles. But, that's not what this scripture is saying. It is saying that this is the foundation for all believers. Now from our perspective, which is far below the foundation level of New Testament faith, we're setting the bar much higher than ever before. But it really isn't me doing this. It isn't us as the church doing this. It is Jesus who has set the bar so high. It's God the Father who has set the bar so high. It's the Holy Spirit that encourages us to move on up! Somehow we've gotten down into the basement of faith and ministry, and have to climb up to the foundation. But, in this last hour before the return of Christ, it is high time for us to begin. In the last few minutes of this last hour, it is time for us to become the disciples Jesus commanded us to be. It's time to step up to the plate of FAITH.

And, now that we're thinking about this, we have to deal with Jesus' question again. "Do you believe this?" And, then there are other big faith questions: Do you believe Jesus or not? Will you obey Jesus or not? This was supposed to be AIT and now you're back in boot-camp. So, what will you do? We shouldn't have to go back to the basics. But we have lost some big games, and now the coach is saying, "OK team, let's go back to the basics. You need to learn and practice the basic skills all over again. You need to get back to playing well at the basic level so you can move back up again. Are you going to be ready for the big game on game day?"

Imagine the glory of God which will be revealed when we live up to these promises. Imagine the glory being raised up to

God when we all begin to believe what Jesus said. Imagine the glory if we all begin to do what Jesus commanded. Imagine the glory which would come to God the Father, if we all obeyed this way and at this level every day. If each of us began to heal the sick, raise the dead, cleanse the lepers, and cast out demons, the world would turn to the church. The world would run to Jesus. The world would bow its knee to the power of God in their midst, and give Him the glory He so richly deserves.

I challenge you to get focused on this new norm. Pray for and receive His resurrection power. After all, it is for you that He did this. But, first, you need a spiritual resurrection for yourself. Then you can call others to be raised with Christ. To God be the glory forever and ever! Amen!

Imagine the joy you will experience in telling others about that resurrection power. That's what we're supposed to be doing. We should be talking about it, doing it, and giving testimonies about the results. Do you believe it enough to preach it? Do you believe it enough to live it?

It's time to move on up to the advanced levels of training. It's time to start obeying our Commander in Chief. It's time to start living the life of faith. No more limitations! Are you ready?

NOTES

SUMMARY

In chapter 2 of the book of acts, we read the powerful story of the fulfillment of one of God's greatest promises. After the resurrection, Jesus basically told the disciples to get into the right place, with the right spirit, in unity, and brace themselves to receive an outpouring of power.

> *"And being assembled together with them, He commanded them not to depart from Jerusalem, but to wait for the Promise of the Father, "which," He said, "you have heard from Me; for John truly baptized with water, but you shall be baptized with the Holy Spirit not many days from now." (Acts 1:4-5)*

In Acts, Chapter 2, we see the fulfillment of that promise from the Father. The disciples had been trained personally by Jesus for three years. They had survived the hardships, persecution, and the loss of their leader on the cross. After the resurrection, they were now ready for more of what God had promised long ago. It took all this preparation to get them in the right place, and in the right frame of mind at the right time. After centuries of celebrating the Day of Pentecost, the Jewish believers were about to receive the promised outpouring of the Holy Spirit with a baptism in fire. The waiting was over, and now it was right in God's timing.

"When the Day of Pentecost had fully come, they were all with one accord in one place.

And suddenly there came a sound from heaven, as of a rushing mighty wind, and it filled the whole house where they were sitting. Then there appeared to them divided tongues, as of fire, and one sat upon each of them. And they were all filled with the Holy Spirit and began to speak with other tongues, as the Spirit gave them utterance." (Acts 2:1-4)

It is difficult to imagine the response of the people that day. The 120 men and women who gathered in that upper room had been completely transformed. They were now more like Jesus than they had imagined possible. The power that had been in Him was now in them. When they took it out into the streets, everyone knew that something major had shifted in the spiritual realm. Look carefully at the response of the crowd outside:

"And there were dwelling in Jerusalem Jews, devout men, from every nation under heaven. And when this sound occurred, the multitude came together, and were confused, because everyone heard them speak in his own language. Then they were all amazed and marveled, saying to one another, "Look, are not all these who speak Galileans? And how is it that we hear, each in our own language in which we were born? Parthians and Medes and Elamites, those dwelling in Mesopotamia, Judea and Cappadocia, Pontus and Asia, Phrygia and Pamphylia, Egypt and the parts of Libya adjoining Cyrene, visitors from Rome, both Jews and proselytes, Cretans and Arabs—we hear them speaking in our own tongues the wonderful works of God." So they were all amazed and perplexed, saying to one another, "Whatever could this mean?" Others mocking said, "They are full of new wine." (Acts 2:5-13)

The writer says that the people were "amazed and per-plexed." I think this is probably an understatement. The amazing thing is that there were some who just didn't get it. They began to make fun of the disciples. And you know that is how some people will respond to you when they see these same gifts operating in your ministry. The people in that day had gotten accustomed to a powerless religion just as people in our day have grown weary and lost confidence in the power of God.

Peter stood up to explain what was happening, and his explanation is as strange as the events going on in the streets of Jerusalem. He begins to explain that this is the fulfillment of something promised by the Lord through the prophet Joel:

> *"But Peter, standing up with the eleven, raised his voice and said to them, "Men of Judea and all who dwell in Jerusalem, let this be known to you, and heed my words. For these are not drunk, as you suppose, since it is only the third hour of the day.*
>
> *But this is what was spoken by the prophet Joel: 'And it shall come to pass in the last days, says God, That I will pour out of My Spirit on all flesh; Your sons and your daughters shall prophesy, Your young men shall see visions, Your old men shall dream dreams. And on My menservants and on My maidservants I will pour out My Spirit in those days; And they shall prophesy. I will show wonders in heaven above And signs in the earth beneath: Blood and fire and vapor of smoke. The sun shall be turned into darkness, And the moon into blood, Before the coming of the great and awesome day of the Lord. And it shall come to pass That whoever calls on the name of the Lord Shall be saved.'"* (Acts 2:14-21)

This is an amazing explanation because it didn't actually explain what they were seeing. They were seeing people who acted drunk and were speaking in languages they could all understand. But, Peter was talking about prophesy, dreams, and visions. Joel proclaimed the Word of the Lord that the Holy Spirit would be poured out on all flesh. However, it was obvious that only the 120 believers had that Spirit on them. Other believers began to receive the Holy Spirit when the apostles laid hands on them. But, even then, it was not on all flesh. It is clear that this outpouring which began on the Day of Pentecost is still moving toward an ultimate fulfillment when "all flesh" will experience it.

This Pentecostal outpouring is still in progress, and I believe this is what God is doing by sending out the "Seven Spirits of God" into the whole world. In our time (the last hour), this outpouring is accelerating. Unprecedented numbers of people are receiving the baptism of the Holy Spirits and the gifts prophesied by Joel. How about you? Are you operating in it, now? If not, are you ready for God to pour out His power in your life, your ministry, and your church through the release of the seven Spirits?

When this power comes in the promised areas of prophesy, visions, and dreams, it will also bring power to many other promises. The promise of Jesus in Luke, Chapter 10, will have the power of God in it to be effective through you. Are you ready to operate in this level of authority?

"And He said to them, "I saw Satan fall like lightning from heaven. Behold, I give you the authority to trample on serpents and scorpions, and over all the power of the enemy, and nothing shall by any means hurt you." (Luke 10:18-19)

When this promise is empowered by the Holy Spirit, we will no longer hear the saints of God testifying to all the damage the enemy is doing to them. We will no longer hear about the devil beating the saints into submission. The world has heard so much of this that they believe the devil is stronger than the Lord. But, we know this is impossible. We need to stop confessing things which contradict the words of our Lord Jesus. He said you have authority "over all the power of the enemy, and nothing shall by any means hurt you." What part of this are we unable to understand? "All" means "all." When the Holy Spirit is poured out on you, you will have authority over "ALL" the power of the enemy. And "nothing" means "nothing." "NOTHING" shall be any means harm you when the seven Spirits of God are working through you.

In closing, I want to strongly urge you to stop being fascinated by evil spirits; stop attributing so much power to them; and stop giving them authority through your confessions. The Bible tells us over 328 times to stop being afraid. So don't be afraid of the enemy. Stand on what James said in the fourth chapter of his letter to believers.

"Therefore submit to God. Resist the devil and he will flee from you. Draw near to God and He will draw near to you. Cleanse your hands, you sinners; and purify your hearts, you double-minded." (James 4:7-8)

PRAYER OF SUBMISSION TO GOD

Father God, I submit to you; spirit, soul, and body. All that I am and all that I ever hope to be; all that I have and all that I will ever have, I submit to you. I resist the devil, and in accordance with your Word and in the mighty name of Jesus he must flee from me. In Jesus' name, Amen and Amen!

Carl Von Clausewitz:
9 Principles of War

Around the time of Napoleon, Carl Von Clausewitz, a brilliant military expert wrote the book, "On War." In this book, he identified nine critically important principles of war. These principles were so well thought out and wisely presented that they are still used in officer training around the world. These principles are:

1. **Mass**: mass your forces for maximum power to defeat the enemy.
2. **Objective**: Clearly identify the primary objective and stay focused on it until it is achieved.
3. **Offensive**: Rather than taking a defensive position, seize the initiative and take the fight to the enemy using surprise where possible.
4. **Maneuver**: Continuously move your forces to positions advantageous to your operations.
5. **Unity of Command**: All forces must be under the command of one single leadership element.

6. **Security**: Protect and defend your positions from enemy infiltration or invasion which would give them the advantage.
7. **Simplicity**: Plans must be simple, clear, and understood at all levels to insure the focus will remain on the primary objective in the fog battle.
8. **Surprise**: Take the battle to the enemy when he least expects it and is least prepared to defend against your assault.
9. **Economy of Force**: Properly align you forces for maximum impact in all areas of the battle.

CPSIA information can be obtained at www.ICGtesting.com
Printed in the USA
243424LV00002B/12/P